D0260919

3 8025 00 13 13 2

Specialist adviser: Dr Peter Moore,
University of Kent at Canterbury

General editors: Jean-Olivier Héron,
Jacqueline Vallon

Editors, English edition: Mary Dortch,
Vanessa Hamilton

*The Publishers gratefully acknowledge the
invaluable help of Douglas Matthews, BA, FLA.*

ISBN 1 85103 096 4

First published 1989 by Editions Gallimard
First published 1991 in Great Britain by Moonlight Publishing Ltd,
36 Stratford Road, London W8
© 1989 Editions Gallimard
English text © 1991 Moonlight Publishing Ltd

Typeset in Great Britain by Technical Art Services
Printed in Italy by La Editoriale Libraria

WORLD
RELIGIONS
PAST AND PRESENT

WRITTEN BY:
Paul Balta, Jean Bottéro, Cathérine Chadefaud,
Charles Chauvin, Sophie Denis, François-Xavier Dillmann,
Henri Fesquet, Louis Frédéric, Charles Gendron,
Edouard Gourévitch, Pierre Grimal, Jean Guiart,
Jean-Olivier Héron, Clarisse Herrenschmidt,
Philippe Jacquin, Jacqueline Kelen, Nicole Maillard,
Jean-Pierre Mohen, Susan Monzon, Eric Navet,
Claude Rivière, Harmut O. Rotermund, Philippe Schlemmer,
Marie-Josèphe Stève, Christian Troubé, Denis Vialou,
Vladimir Vodoff, Hyacinthe Vulliez, Wang Chia-Yu,
Slimane Zéghidour.

ILLUSTRATED BY:
Elisabeth Bogaert, Paul Bontemps, Frédéric Clément,
Manne Héron, Gilbert Houbre, Pierre de Hugo,
Daniel Moignot, Sylvaine Pérols, Jean-Yves Poirier,
Jean-Marie Poissenot, James Prunier, Catherine Ripoll,
Christian Rivière, Pascal Robin, Saladin, Jean-Claude Senée
Etienne Souppart, Valérie Stetten, Dominique Thibault.

TRANSLATED BY:
Professor John Fletcher, Beryl Fletcher,
Sarah Matthews, Penny Stanley-Baker

MOONLIGHT PUBLISHING

Contents

Religions
through time

30,000 BC: Mother goddess cult.
10,000 BC: Polytheism and animism.

3000 BC: Sumerians invent writing.
2400 BC: Pharaoh's Egypt.
  Megalithic culture in northern Europe (Stonehenge).

2000 BC: Cretan civilization.
1700 BC: Babylonian Empire.

500–400 BC: Greek golden age.
AD 30: Crucifixion of Christ under Roman Empire.

70: Destruction of the temple in Jerusalem

250–900: Mayan civilization.
315: Roman Emperor Constantine converts to Christianity.

c. 500: Celtic religion disappears

1100–1300: Great European cathedrals built.
1200: Maori religion (Oceania).

1200: Inca civilization (site of Machu Picchu).
1229: Inquisition.

15th century: Europeans in Africa (slave trade).
First Dalai Lama in Tibet.

19th century: Missionaries in Africa.
1905: Separation of Church and State in France.

1917: Bolshevik Revolution in Russia. Marxism triumphs.
1933: Rise of Nazism in Germany. Beginning of extermination of Jews.

1947: Gandhi. Indian independence.

> *The power of God is revealed*
> *in a million different forms.*
> Any, Egyptian scribe, *c.* 1650 BC

1500 BC: Vedic religion in India.
1300 BC: Monotheism develops (Moses).

1000 BC: Olmec civilization, Mexico.
850–780 BC: Homer (*Iliad* and *Odyssey*).

700 BC: Zoroaster in Persia.
490 BC: Lao-tze (China) founder of Taoism.
553–433 BC: The Buddha (India).

551 BC: Confucius in China.

570–632: Muhammad.
700: Arab conquest of Africa and Spain.

962: Holy Roman Empire.
1100: Khmer kingdom, Angkor-Vat built.

1100: Aztec civilization.
1056: Beginning of the Crusades.

53: Fall of Constantinople, capital of the Eastern Christian Empire.
21: Luther's break with Rome.

1533: Anglican Church breaks with Rome.

1562–1593: French wars of religion.
1793: French Revolution, cult of the Goddess Reason.

1962: Pope John XXIII opens the second Vatican Council.
1966: In China, Mao heads the Cultural Revolution.

1979: Ayatollah Khomeini founds the Islamic Republic of Iran.

1988: Pope John Paul II brings together the heads of the major religions.

9

Religions round the world

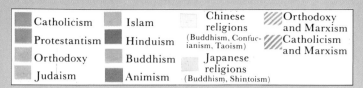

			Chinese religions (Buddhism, Confucianism, Taoism)	Orthodoxy and Marxism
Catholicism	Islam			Catholicism and Marxism
Protestantism	Hinduism			
Orthodoxy	Buddhism			
Judaism	Animism	Japanese religions (Buddhism, Shintoism)		

THE COMMON CORE

What is religion?

When it was thought that rivers were inhabited by gods and nymphs, a priest asked their permission before building a bridge across. Priests thus came to be called bridge-makers, or pontiffs (from the Latin *pons*). The knots of straw (*religio*) holding the bridges together may be the origin for our word 'religion'.

Mysterious beginnings

Religions deal with the mysteries at the heart of life: how life began, what is the meaning of life, what happens when we die. The word 'religion' is itself a little mysterious. Nobody quite knows where it comes from. It may come from the Latin *religio* which means worry or scruple, or straw, or it may come from *religare*, to link or tie together.

How the Bible explains the beginning of the world, according to a 14th century manuscript.

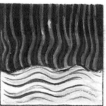

In the beginning, chaos

The creation of the heavens

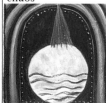

The creation of plants ...

... planets, animals and people

14

This idea of linking is important, since religion is the link between the world we know and see, and the unseen world of spirits which needs to be soothed and wooed. Religion is the link between people who share the same beliefs and have the same values. Religion links the present to the past through traditional beliefs and practices, customs and stories. Whatever the real root of the word, the idea of linking is perhaps the most appropriate and revealing.

Sometimes, though, religion can become a barrier instead of a link, setting people apart instead of joining them together. All through history different religions have been used by political leaders as a way of ensuring their own political position by setting one people, one faith, against another.

A Western Buddhist ceremony

Gathering together men and women who share particular beliefs and values, religions set up societies which are more or less rigidly organized. The beliefs may be in one god or several gods, but they may also be in abstract ideas such as the notion of goodness or the remembrance of those who have died. It is not necessary to believe in a god to be religious.

What happens after we die? The ancient Egyptians carried out elaborate rituals to ensure their survival in an afterlife. All wealthy Egyptians ensured that, on their death, their bodies were embalmed and placed in an elaborate tomb, surrounded by servants who would wait on them in the world to come.

15

Only a madman looks at the finger which is pointing out the moon.
Chinese proverb

Incense and light play subtly on our senses and are used in all kinds of rituals from those of ancient Mesopotamia to Hindu, Buddhist, Jewish or Christian rituals today.

Throughout this book, we are going to be a bit like the madman in the Chinese proverb, *looking at the finger and not at what it is pointing to*. Each religion's character is different and each individual's faith personal and unique. But certain ways of thinking and acting are shared between people and by most religions. The ideas held in common can be expressed in signs and symbols.

What is a sign?

If you write down a + like this, then that is a written sign for the word 'plus', which is itself only an audible or visual sign for the idea of addition. The sound 'plus' and the sign + are two physical representations of an idea which has no physical reality.

For many Africans, the special, all-pervasive religious aspects of life are expressed spontaneously in dance.

It is impossible to transmit an idea of anything that we see, hear or understand without expressing it through the means of one sign or another. That is why religions, which deal with concepts, with non-physical realities, use physical means to make them visible and accessible: symbols, gestures, scents, music, objects, even foods.

By making the invisible a physical presence, religions attempt to tame the unknown, illuminate mysteries and offer people the opportunity to come into contact with that invisible presence which they sometimes experience as a sense deep within themselves.

The ringing of a bell, made up of every sound, is very dear to the god of gods. The ringing of a bell carries as much merit as ten thousand sacrifices.

Skanda-Purana II, 6

An Egyptian musician playing hymns on his harp to the sun-god, Ra (*c.* 1000 BC)

Music, like all other arts, has its origins in religion. Many religions see all human art and technology as having divine origins.

It is customary to ring a bell when going into a Hindu temple. Not only does the bell frighten off evil spirits, but it also catches the god's attention.

What does 'sacred' mean?

If you say that something is sacred, you mean that for you it belongs to a higher or a better world, it inspires total respect. Thus the sacred thing becomes different, set apart from other things that may be physically similar. It has an *otherness* – something special – about it.

In this way, the sacred crocodile which used to float idly in the pools of the temple in the City of Crocodiles, at the time of the Pharaohs, was no different from his muddy brothers on the banks of the Nile, unless you saw him as representing the sun itself ... In which case that crocodile would become unique,

The word 'profane' comes from the Latin pro fanum, meaning outside the holy ground of the temple.

The fierce and sometimes terrifying statues guarding Buddhist temples in Japan remind those approaching of all the obstacles to be overcome before they can reach the ultimate happiness of Nirvana.

Offerings being made to Sebek, the crocodile-headed god of the Nile, 900 BC

an animal apart from all ordinary crocodiles in the world.

If the one crocodile is sacred, then the others are separated from it by their lack of sanctity. In this way, people separate the holy from the profane. The holy – the sacred – is the domain of the gods; the profane is the everyday world.

Chinese characters representing the centre of the sacred space, in a Taoist temple.

A medieval reliquary of Charlemagne, made to contain bones or clothing of a saint. Reliquaries were thought to protect their wearers. They were a physical manifestation of the sacred.

Although people live in the ordinary or profane world, the fact that there are sacred areas, holy places, gives us reference points, boundaries, goals. Each one of us has our own sense of obligation to whatever we consider sacred: our country, our freedom, our rights, our loved ones, our beliefs.

Muslims prostrating themselves before Muhammad as shown in a 17th century miniature. Muhammad, the prophet of Allah, can only be painted veiled. The saintly, the sacred, belongs to a world which is *other* and cannot be painted.

19

The gods

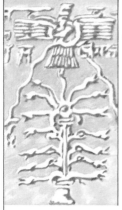

Whether referred to in the singular or plural, with a capital G or without, a god could be said to be a supreme being with particular functions, and power over people's lives. In a way, one could say that a god is the answer to a question that could not have had any other answer at the time. Why, for instance, is there thunder and lightning?

On the left, you can see the Mesopotamian god, Assur, sending rain down on the earth, making it fertile and full of life.

The Hindu god Shiva and his wife Parvati (who represents his creative energy). Shiva is both creator and destroyer – destroying in order to create anew. He has five heads, which represent his five aspects, and ten arms, representing the ten directions of space. On each arm a hand holds a symbol of the god's power. A third eye on his forehead is the sign of Perfect knowledge. (after a 17th century painting)

He is One and Indivisible, but seems to divide into all forms and all creatures, and to appear as every distinct form of creation. All things are eternally born from him, and are eternally recalled into his eternity.
Bhagavad-Gita, 13 : 17

Because Zeus hurls them about the sky, thought the Ancient Greeks. Why is the world full of violence and death? Because, say the Hindus, Shiva has unleashed them. Who makes the fields fertile? Baal, of course, the Canaanites would have said. Others would say the Earth Mother, the Dragon or the Sacred Goat.

For the Hindus, the god, Surya, is the sun. He crosses the sky in a chariot drawn by seven horses, or by one horse with seven heads. All Hindus start the day by praying to him. (after a 17th century miniature)

But personification is neither stupid nor misleading. Worshipping gods is a way of saying that nature and feelings are connected with an invisible reality which is greater than human understanding. The gods represent the forces of order and disorder in the world.

Thus, human nature and life are filled with the presence of divine protectors who can be wooed by carrying out particular rites and rituals. If they have not been won over, they may become jealous, mischief-making enemies.

Shualuo, or the Old Man of the South Pole, decides the length of a person's life, according to Chinese mythology.

God

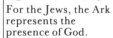

For the Jews, the Ark represents the presence of God.

The names of God

To name something is, in some ways, to own it. Human beings cannot possess God, and so they cannot name Him. The Bible puts His name into a code of four consonants (see p.141), or uses a host of other terms: the Most High, the Eternal, the Lord, the Almighty ...

God in the singular, with a capital G, is the Other, that which cannot be named nor understood. He is much more of a question than He is an answer.

Human beings live in time; they can no more imagine a being who lives outside time, in eternity, than a baby in its mother's womb can imagine her face. According to the Bible, God has made Himself known to human beings through Abraham and his descendants, and has formed a relationship of mutual love with mankind.

For those who believe in many gods and demons, the world is a crowded, busy place. For the *monotheist*, a believer in a single God, there is the one relationship, freely entered into in love and trust.

Through that relationship the Jewish people can find in their history an understanding, not only of God, but also of mankind. That understanding is still being worked out by the descendants of Abraham: Jews, Christians or Muslims.

Western Christians alone show God in pictures, often representing Him by a hand coming from the clouds. The hand of God reaches out for the hand of Jesus – God and man, the visible image of the Father. (9th century manuscript)

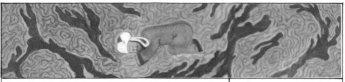

Judaism and Islam alike forbid pictures of God. Here Muhammad is shown in the presence of Allah, surrounded by a blazing light.

For Christians, God is both One and Three: Father, Son and Holy Ghost, in the same way that the spring, the stream and the estuary all make up the single reality of the river.

God ruling over the world and the universe (15th century manuscript)

What is a believer?

Philosophy is the study of the truths underlying all knowledge and reality, confining itself to that which can be described through reasoning.

The Buddha had four meetings (with an old man, a sick man, a dead man and a wise man), which decided him to seek a cure for all the world's ills. Meditation on the limits of existence encourages Buddhists to follow the Buddha's example.

A believer has convictions based on experience that is beyond the realm of the everyday. The belief *transcends* ordinary or scientific rules. Holding certain things to be true, some believers

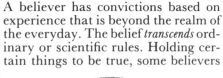

Up to the 14th century, Western Christianity represented the world according to its religion, with Jerusalem at its centre.

are prepared to worship deities, however improbable, to behave according to rules, and even, in the name of these truths, to kill or be killed. For thousands of years, this kind of belief, or faith, has been taken for granted, yet nowadays it often appears as if religion and science are in conflict with each other.

Religion and science For an ancient Egyptian, the god Osiris was responsible for the fertility of the land. Nowadays, he would give credit to fertilisers, but would also thank Osiris for the discovery of fertilisers.

For a believer, there is no conflict. Scientific discoveries simply describe one aspect of reality. For a believer, the universe is like a book; one can measure the length of the lines, scrutinise the letters, analyse the ink and the paper, but none of these reaches beyond the materials used in the book to the meaning of the text. For a believer, all things have a meaning; all you have to do is know how to read. So say all religions, and those who teach us to read reality are the prophets, wise men, gurus, sorcerers, shamans.

The apostle Thomas did not believe that Jesus had risen from the dead, and asked to touch his wounds. (from an 11th century sculpture) *Jesus saith unto him, Thomas, because thou hast seen me, thou hast believed: blessed are they who have not seen, and yet have believed.* St John, 20 : 29

Seeing Jesus walk upon the water, Peter, his disciple, went to meet him, but grew afraid: *Jesus stretched forth his hand, and caught him, and said unto him, O thou of little faith, wherefore didst thou doubt?* St Matthew, 14 : 31

25

What is prayer?

Before beginning their prayers, Muslims stand to affirm the greatness of Allah (from a 16th century miniature)

Religions do not simply deal with answers to man's questions about the origin and meaning of life which have been asked since the beginning of time. Nor do religions confine themselves to defining only good and evil.

Religions also cope with people's fear of the unknown, and with their need to love and to be loved. They provide a response to people's desire for perfection, their longing for peace and harmony and happiness, their need for comfort and their wish to have someone to thank for all that is beautiful.

The manner in which people pray differs, depending on their traditions.

Prayer is a conversation between the intellect and God... He who loves God is constantly in conversation with Him as with a Father... When, through prayer, you have reached a point beyond all other happiness, then, in truth, you will have found prayer.
Evagrius the Pontic,
4th century Christian

Buddhist from Ladakh

Muslim

Ancient Egyptian

Ancient Greek

26

Prayer springs from all these different aims, needs and desires. It is a way of turning towards a *presence* and entering into some kind of relationship with it. People praying both offer and receive. They may offer praise, requests, thanks, or simply contemplation and peaceful adoration. They may use words, songs, or silence; they may move and gesture, or remain still; they may use physical objects, scents, lights and other symbols. In exchange, they receive – or believe they receive – all kinds of blessings. The ties thus woven between the visible and the invisible work towards their own well-being and towards the harmony of the world.

People who pray sometimes reach a state of ecstasy where they are apparently carried out of themselves, entranced by whatever it is they have been contemplating or calling on. In these trance-like conditions, people may do all sorts of extraordinary things, which simply remind us how little we understand the laws of nature and of the human mind.

Picture of a person praying (from a 3rd century Roman catacomb)

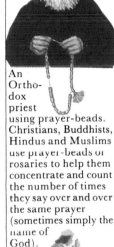

An Ortho-dox priest using prayer-beads. Christians, Buddhists, Hindus and Muslims use prayer-beads or rosaries to help them concentrate and count the number of times they say over and over the same prayer (sometimes simply the name of God).

Buddhist

Tibetan Buddhist

Christian

Muslim

What is a ritual?

Ritual washing is carried out in different ways according to different religions, but it is a part of most of them. The picture above shows ritual washing according to Muslim custom. (from a 15th century miniature)

Imagine declaring your love by offering a bouquet of flowers. If one flower from that bouquet were pressed between the pages of a book, it could represent, fifty years later, the whole history and intensity of that love. But if some stranger opened the book and saw the flower, to them it would be meaningless—nothing but faded petals.

Whether it is love or religion, emotions fade from their first intensity, but scents and sounds and objects can, like the sight of a pressed flower, bring that first rush of feeling flooding back. So religions use words and gestures and objects as a way back to their central meaning, as a springboard for prayer.

In Mongolia, stone cairns still indicate places where it is best to sacrifice a horse or perform some other ritual to please the spirits.

28

Over a period of time, a web of agreed signs and conventions gradually builds up to become a body of *rituals*. They are based on what first happened spontaneously, then was repeated frequently enough to be preserved for ever. In the Christian church, the communion service or Eucharist re-enacts for the believer the last supper when Christ broke and ate bread with his disciples. Rituals are the collective memory of the community of believers; they transmit its meaning to new generations.

Rituals make use of symbols, such as incense, oil, wine, and objects such as statues. Sometimes, though, the symbols are confused with what they stand for: the statues are worshipped for themselves, not for the divinity they represent. They become idols.

Declaration of Faith, according to the Catholic tradition: the white clothes, the candles, the entire ritual, serve to emphasise and make visible the promises that are being made.

A **liturgy** is a form of public worship of a divinity or saint. Taking the collective prayer, it gives it shape through gestures, readings, chants, symbols and ritual movements.

In Beijing, the Emperors of China celebrated the rituals of the seasons in the Temple of the Sky; in the 15th century a pagoda was built around the temple to hold the sacred texts used in the rituals.

Festivals

Whether they are sad or joyful, solemn or lively, festivals are a break in the monotony of daily life, a doorway to something that never dies – the eternal. That is why religions, whose role it is

Many traditions represent life hereafter as an eternal festival. Here you can see the Eight Immortals of Taoism (p. 234), wise men who have met together in eternity.

Masks are often used in sacred dances. They allow dancers to represent divinities and to give them a physical presence. In this way, modern Buddhist monks in Tibet and Bhutan re-enact episodes from their religious history.

The Dogon, who live in Mali, Africa, often have a masked dancer on stilts to perform at funerals. He shows to the dead pictures of the world they have left.

to put people in touch with that mysterious something, consider festivals important: full moon, solstices, rain, sunshine, seedtime, harvest, birth, marriage, death, war, peace, various anniversaries – all are pretexts for festivals. Festivals take place throughout the year, symbols of the eternal festival that religions promise us in the after-life.

Celebrate the festival of your god, starting afresh each time the moment comes round again. God becomes angry should he be overlooked... Songs, dances and incense are as food to him, and those who prostrate themselves before him become his wealth. God will magnify the name of the one who does so, and the person will become as drunk.

Egyptian advice, 16th century BC

The Hindus have hosts of gods, and hosts of festivals. The festivals are full of colour: dance, music, masks, processions of huge chariots carrying statues of the gods, escorted by heavily decorated elephants and a crowd of pilgrims.

All religious festivals... consist of a re-enactment of a holy moment which first occurred in a mythical time.

Mircea Eliade

3

Offerings and Sacrifices

Offerings of flowers are a Hindu ritual or *puja*.

Giving members of our family presents is fun, but to have a real understanding of the presents or offerings that people give in their religions, it is necessary to go back in time. In ancient times, people tried to avoid misfortune by making friends with those powers who controlled life and death – in other words, the gods.

How could they make the gods their friends, though? By organizing festivals in their honour, and sharing meals with them in a symbolic way: libations of wine, milk and oil, offerings of cereals, vegetables, fruit, flowers and animals, presents, tributes, and sacrifices such as the firstborn son or the firstborn of the flock.

Some rituals moved from offering objects to offering obedience:
I delight not in the blood of bullocks, or of lambs, or of he goats...
Put away the evil of your doings from before mine eyes; cease to do evil.
Isaiah, 1 : 11-16

An offering of grapes, flowers and cakes painted on the wall of an Egyptian tomb, about 15th century BC

Christians join with God in taking communion, which commemorates and re-enacts Christ's sacrifice of himself to save mankind. Through the symbolism of the Eucharist, believers try to model themselves on him.

Blessed be Thy name, O Lord, who hast given us this bread, the fruit of the fields and of man's labour. We here offer it to you: it will become the bread of life.

Ritual of the Mass

An Aztec priest offers a victim's heart to a god.

Aztec sacrificial stone knife

In the Aztec religion, it was thought that blood spilt during human sacrifice was drunk by the sun, which was restored by it and grew in strength so that it could, in turn, restore and revive the whole of creation. Both priests and victims were seen as being divine.

Blood spilt has taken on the symbolism of a sacrifice, making atonement and obtaining blessings in a way that gives a positive meaning to sorrow and death.

In traditional African beliefs, the living remained in communion with the dead. They would ask for their advice, offering them a sacrifice (in this case, a chicken), so that they could drink its reviving blood. In quite another part of the world, and thousands of years ago, Ulysses, the ancient Greek hero, sacrificed animals before asking the gods' advice.

Sacred Animals

In Hindu mythology, the gods are carried by particular animals which symbolize them. The bird Garuda is ridden by the god, Vishnu, or by one of his incarnations. Here, Krishna, an incarnation of Vishnu, and Radha, are mounted on Garuda, the enemy of the Nagas, the gods of water. He is the flying word, symbol of the sacred texts of the Vedas (p. 202).

The buffalo usually appears to be sunk in thought; the cow, feeding people with her milk, watches after the welfare of her calves. People cannot resist attributing to animals their own feelings, faults and virtues, and it is easy to see how particular animals have become associated with particular characteristics.

For instance, it was because jackals are scavengers of dead bodies that the ancient Egyptians made them guardians of the dead under the name of the god Anubis. At the same time, the fertile ram lent his form to Knum, the Egyptian god of creation.

Imdugud, the lion-headed eagle, storm-god of the Mesopotamians (p. 64), is shown flanked by two deer, symbols of fertility (temple gateway, near Ur).

Dragons are often shown as guardians of treasure or of sacred places. The dragons symbolize the obstacles which have to be overcome in order to reach them.

According to Jewish tradition, the dove is the embodiment of purity, hope and peace. For Christians, it is also the symbol of the Holy Spirit.
...he saw the heavens opened and the Spirit like a Dove descending upon him.
St Mark, 1 : 10

Cows are associated with the earth, the source of nourishment (p. 43). Cows are still revered in India:
The Cow is the Sky, the Cow is the Earth ... in her lies the divine order, and Holiness. ... That is all that beholds the Sun.
Atharva Veda

Then, over the centuries, as people placed a greater value on what was human, these representations of the gods lost all their animal features, except those which expressed their particular attribute, or characteristic.

In this way, Hathor, the gentle cow, goddess of Love and Birth, kept only her cow's horns as a sign. Except for these, she has the face and body of a woman. As for Anubis, Thut and Knum, they kept their animal heads and were given human bodies.

The garden of the gods

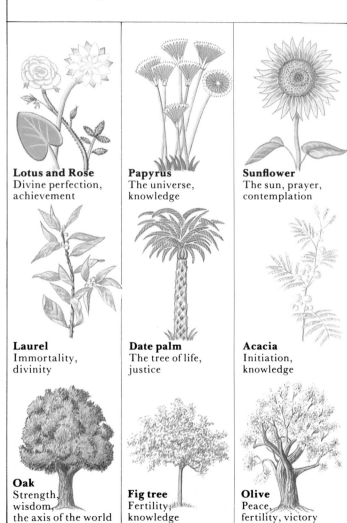

Lotus and Rose
Divine perfection,
achievement

Papyrus
The universe,
knowledge

Sunflower
The sun, prayer,
contemplation

Laurel
Immortality,
divinity

Date palm
The tree of life,
justice

Acacia
Initiation,
knowledge

Oak
Strength,
wisdom,
the axis of the world

Fig tree
Fertility,
knowledge

Olive
Peace,
fertility, victory

Chrysanthemum
The sun, perfection, immortality

Vine
The tree of life, rebirth

Banyan tree
Strength, life

Mistletoe
Rebirth, immortality

Maize and Wheat
The gift of life, prosperity

Cypress, pine
Immortality

Forests are natural sanctuaries. They are places that are ideal for making contact with the supernatural.

Trees form a link between the world below and that above. *Trees, eternal attempts by the earth / to speak to the listening sky.*
  Rabindranath Tagore

Trees thrust their roots down into the soil, then reach upwards to the sky. Their leaves and branches extend to the sun and wind. Their flowers ripen into fruit. Grass and crops feed us. Plants heal us, and can poison us. Plants waft beautiful scents, some of which give us visions: the entire vegetable kingdom tells people something about the mystery of creation. Because of this, plants play an important part in rites and rituals and sacred sayings, whether they be the mistletoe which grows without ever touching the ground, or the lotus.

Messengers

It is a basic religious impulse to set up lines of communication between this world and the unknown world beyond.

And [Jacob] dreamed, and behold a ladder set up on the earth, and the top of it reached to heaven: and behold the angels of God ascending and descending on it.

Genesis, 28 : 12

All these ladders, magic trees, holy mountains, all these means of flying through the air, from the Jewish prophet Elias' flaming chariot to the winged sandals of the Greek god, Hermes, God's angels and Muhammad's mare, show that the gulf between humanity and the gods might indeed be crossed.

Religions set up intermediaries between the sacred and the profane, intermediaries which, rising from the earth and reaching down from the sky, touch and meet, like stalactites and stalagmites. The columns which are thus built are believed to hold the world in balance. Those who rise from the earth are grounded in the common people, and climb up to the king, who is sometimes thought to be a living god. Between these two extremes comes a host of priests or prophets, seers, wise men and those initiated

The route leading to the world of the gods, where all will go after they die, is often represented by a ladder. Only the blessed and initiates can scale the ladder, all others are pitched down below.

Charon, the Greek ferryman, rowed the dead across the river to Hades, the abode of the dead. (after J. Patinir, 16th century)

The Buddha is shown climbing down a ladder to teach the way to salvation. (Indian sculpture of the 2nd to 5th centuries)

Shamans or sorcerers appear to make frequent journeys to where the gods dwell, in search of the means to heal or soothe the people in their care. To make their journeys they use different means such as drugs and dancing. The Siberian Altais use the soul of a sacrificed horse as a vehicle, and have to go through various ordeals before they can reach the god they wish to question or ask for help.

into formal rites.

Allah has sent to his creatures a Messenger to guide them to Him and that Messenger has left behind, after his death, successors to re- place him in his task of guide towards Allah.

Al-Ghazali

The world beyond is, according to different religions, inhabited by differ- ent ranks of gods and goddesses. These consist of demons and messengers, as well as the millions of intermediaries and interceders such as the saints, the blessed, martyrs, and the enormous number of guardian ancestors.

Some monarchs base their power on their 'divine' connection. Hirohito, who died in 1989, was known as the 124th God-Emperor of Japan.

Rainbows are often seen as a manifest- ation of the divine, a bridge between the human world and the world of the divine. They are also seen by some as the sun and rain linked together, a promise of fertility.

39

What is a priest?

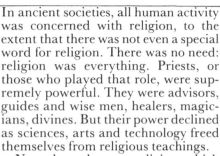

A Mayan warrior-priest (7th century sculpture). His feathered head-dress shows his relation with the priests' god Quetzalcoatl (p. 113).

Mesopotamian priest (Carving from 8th century BC)

In ancient societies, all human activity was concerned with religion, to the extent that there was not even a special word for religion. There was no need: religion was everything. Priests, or those who played that role, were supremely powerful. They were advisors, guides and wise men, healers, magicians, divines. But their power declined as sciences, arts and technology freed themselves from religious teachings.

Nowadays, there are religions which do not have consecrated priests, but in every society there are people who fulfil those functions.

What are their functions?

First and foremost, a priest is a mediator. Standing at the border between the visible and the invisible, he is both the representative of the higher powers before humanity, and the representative of humanity before the higher powers. As a servant of the god, he is also minister of the cult, interpreter of the law and guardian of tradition. As a servant of humanity, he offers to the gods the praises, requests and offerings of the faithful; he intercedes on their behalf, a bridge of souls between this world and the world beyond.

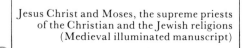

Jesus Christ and Moses, the supreme priests of the Christian and the Jewish religions (Medieval illuminated manuscript)

Rare today, the Christian festival of Rogation took place over the three days leading up to Ascension Day. Its aim was to call God's blessing down on the fruits of the earth and the labours of men. This 19th century painting shows the blessing of a cornfield.

The mythical rainbow snake, of the Aborigines of northern Australia, plays an essential role in fertility. It often appears on Aboriginal bark paintings.

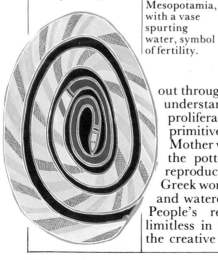

Gudea, god of Mesopotamia, with a vase spurting water, symbol of fertility.

Human life depends on the fertility of the soil. But a hailstorm, a cold snap, the rains failing, a swarm of locusts, or any other of a hundred natural happenings can suddenly lead to disaster where there was promise, bringing starvation to flocks and people.

So, the first duty of so-called primitive religions is to seek to control the fertility of the soil, to promote the vigorous growth of plants, the reproduction of animals, the fecundity of women and the power of men, honoured by the number of their offspring. And so, the first duty of each religion is the promotion and defence of life in every form.

That duty is carried out through fertility rites. So we can understand why there is such a proliferation of sexual images in primitive religions, from the Earth Mother with a hundred breasts, to the pottery phalluses (the male reproductive organ) which ancient Greek women planted in their fields and watered as if they were plants. People's religious imagination is limitless in their desire to stimulate the creative energy of the gods. It is

Fertility rites

also understandable that there should be such particular attention paid to puberty, that period in human life

Two triangles, linked together, reversed and form a fertility symbol which was much used in ancient times. It survives today in Hinduism and in Judaism, where it is called the Star of David

Cretan bull

The Egyptian cow-goddess Hathor

where a boy becomes capable of fertilizing and a girl of being fertilized. This change is often expressed through initiation rites which mark the death of the child and the birth of the adult.

Nowadays, marriage ceremonies and festivals such as Rogation Day can be seen as the contemporary continuation of practices which go back to the beginning of time.

Cows' horns are associated with the moon, a symbol of fertility, with the vital strength of the Earth Mother, and the great fertility goddess. They are frequently depicted.

Decoration from Cretan palaces

Death and beyond

People know that they must die, and so try to come to terms with what they cannot avoid. Religion helps them before, after and during that last journey.

It helps people before they die by telling them what to expect at the end of the journey: for some, the journey is a return trip (reincarnation), for others, it is a one-way trip to another form of life or, for religions based on the Bible, it is a place of waiting, ready for the final resurrection.

During the journey, priests, or those who take their place, present a defence of the dead person before the powers from the world beyond and make the last rites over the body.

After the journey, funeral rites reassure and comfort the bereaved, enabling them to resume their daily life.

Religious rites honour the dead by attempting to prevent eventual decay of the body, either by concealing it (shrouds, sarcophagi, coffins), by mummifying or embalming it, or by destroying it (cremation, devouring, immersion).

Ancient Egyptian mourners

In Indonesia, the Torajas place effigies of their dead outside the graves, dug out of the cliff face.

Left-hand page, the Beyond after a painting by the Flemish painter Hieronymus Bosch (15th century)

The resurrection of Christ represents for Christians the promise of their own ultimate resurrection (from a 13th century fresco)

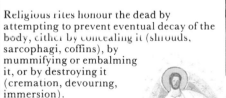

Holy places

The Hittites (p. 88) worshipped a god of the elements and a mountain-god (13th century BC carving)

The Ganges, the most sacred river in India, is the goddess Ganga, who has come down from heaven. To prevent the waters from crushing the world, Shiva caught them in his top-knot. (18th century painting)

Places in the natural world

It is widely believed that there are a great number of meeting points (p.38) between the worlds of the visible and the invisible. People feel in certain places that they can enter into communication with the forces around them. **Mountains**, for instance, formed by the earth itself, reach towards heaven, a heaven which can be imagined as reaching down to them through the clouds. Climbing a mountain, and leaving the ordinary world behind, can be compared with mounting to Heaven, where invisible spirits dwell. **Volcanoes** are at once openings into the regions below (hell, the domain of the dead) and stepping-stones for the celestial powers.

The sea can give life and take it away. To go by sea is to steer between life and death.

There are the living, the dead and those who voyage upon the sea.

Herodotus, *c.*485–426 BC

The Greeks and Romans sacrificed bulls and horses to the sea. More recently, the Doge of Venice would fling his gold ring into the lagoon to symbolize the marriage of his city with the sea.

Rivers, life-bearing, are seen as the symbol of the gods' body. An overflow can be a sign of either his blessing (in the case of the Nile), or of his anger (floods).

The desert faces people with silence, solitude and thirst. It makes them realize their fragility and provides a space to be alone with their gods.

The banyan tree, with its aerial roots, seems like a forest all on its own, peopled with spirits— a striking image of the power of immortality.

The desert faces man with himself and with his god.

Sacred rock in Burma, covered in gold leaf, a place of prayer and pilgrimage for Buddhists.

Strangely-shaped rocks, huge isolated trees, meteorites, lakes, springs, caves, mysterious woods anything odd or out of the ordinary in the natural world makes people think of a divine intention.

Mountains, the earth's despairing gestures before the unreachable.
Rabindranath Tagore

47

*Only the people sacrificed in high places,
because there was no house built unto
the name of the Lord, until those days.*
1 Kings, 3:2

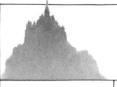

In the 12th century, in France, Benedictine monks built a monastery on top of a rocky island, now known as Mont-Saint-Michel.

A Hindu temple carved out of the rock, a real rocky sanctuary.

And God went up from him in the place where he talked with him. And Jacob set up a pillar in the place where he talked with him, even a pillar of stone: and he poured a drink offering thereon.

Genesis, 35 : 13-14

Man-made places

If mountains provide a special meeting point between people and the kingdom of the gods, then those who live on plains must build their own mountains, so that they too can reach up to their gods. Barrows, pyramids, ziggurats are all conceived for the purpose of reaching upwards. Similarly, the simple altar provides a tiny space lifted out of the ordinary, off well-trodden ground, where the believer can make his offering. Pyramids were even constructed on top of mountains, with altars on top of the pyramids.

Stones raised in Saudi Arabia around 4000 BC. When they were first put up they would have been vertical and parallel. Stone worship was common amongst the ancient Semitic peoples (p. 80).

But the first traces of sacred architecture date much farther back than the early pyramids. They are found in prehistoric sepulchres, neolithic cave-temples, and in the standing stones, steles, totems and other sacred poles raised up into the sky just like the minarets and steeples which we see around us.

As soon as a sacred place has been identified, it becomes a focus of activity. It needs to be sheltered, enclosed, protected from anything

The pyramid at Chichen Itza is 30 m high. It was built by the Mayas a thousand years ago.

that might profane it.

In some holy places, separate buildings are constructed as dwellings for the gods and for those who serve them. Churches and mosques, though, are not so much the dwelling-place of God as houses of prayer for the use of the faithful.

On the plains of America, Indians marked out a medicine-place to converse with the gods.

Caves seem to have been holy places to prehistoric people. They covered them with paintings of unknown meaning. The caves at Pech-Merle, in the Dordogne, are decorated with hand-prints and spotted ponies.

The divine presence is found inside houses too, which is why the believer often keeps a space apart to carry out rituals. That space may be as small as a prayer rug.

The Law

The wheel symbolizes the Buddhist law or dhamma. When a Buddhist begins to pray, he sets the wheel in motion.

He who wishes to find salvation and to be numbered amongst the elect always venerates the holy Law in memory of the teachings of Buddha.
Samyutta nikaya, 1 : 4

People depend for their security – their existence – on belonging to a group with which they can identify. Every group is bound together by rules, the law, to which it conforms. The law establishes a harmony between the needs of the individual and those of the community. It sets down a way of life.

Laws map the path to be taken through life, since law points out what will kill, and what will enhance life. Chaos, anarchy, madness, lack of control, can lead to death; what leads to life is what encourages the best in people: ensuring life is the basis of law.

For religions, life and the way it is best lived derive from the same divine source, and so, the law is laid down in the name of God or the gods. In traditional societies, divine law rules every aspect of life: what you eat, whom you meet, how you worship.

If you break the Law, you expose yourself to divine punishment in the life hereafter. Here, Saint Michael and Satan weigh the souls of the dead.

It governs social life and regulates the punishment of criminals.

Gradually spiritual and worldly powers grew farther apart, as freedom of thought developed. It had become secular, or separated from the Church. Yet there still are today states ruled in the name of God. These are theocracies.

Even in countries with no state religion, people still obey the law in the name of some greater good.

Taboos. Pangolins are an example of something quite out of the ordinary. They have four legs but the scales of a fish. They lay eggs, yet give suck to their young. They have been declared taboo, and outlawed, by the Lele of the Congo. In the same way, bodies decaying, incest, which disrupts the family, are taboo. Things that are taboo are forbidden because they cause confusion.

51

Good and Evil

In Islamic tradition, the angel Gabriel is called Jibril. Good angels are seen as having remained faithful servants of God, while the fallen angels gathered under Iblis (corresponding to Lucifer or Satan).

Amongst all the eternal questions for which religions seek an answer, perhaps the most difficult is that of evil. If goodness and happiness are the central aim and meaning of life, why then does there exist a malevolent power bent on destroying goodness and happiness?

Why is there cruelty, illness, suffering and death? Are these punishments? But, if so, why should the innocent suffer too? Why do we inflict suffering on ourselves? Does evil exist in us all? There are times when everything appears so appalling that it seems there must be some nightmare-god who delights in destroying us and our world. Perhaps that is why some of the oldest responses to the question of evil show the gods destroying the whole human race because of its wickedness (as in the story of the Flood) – a reason why the anger of the gods needs to be placated through rituals (p. 32).

From the 10th to the 13th centuries, Christians carried on a Holy War, a Crusade, against the Moslems, whom they saw as evil.

52

In the Bible, Satan, or the Adversary, is the representative of evil.

But there are other ways of responding to the problems of evil and sin. Buddhists invite people to free themselves from desire, which they see as the root of suffering. For Jews, pain and evil are part of God's teaching: God allows them for the sake of the conversion which will then lead to happiness. There are all sorts of very different responses, but all provide answers or allies: Christians believe that God has saved the world through his son Jesus, who overcame sin and evil.

The Navajo Indians of North America paint in sand as part of their healing rituals. A sick child is placed on the painting to be in contact with the gods.

In Old Testament times, the Jews sent a scapegoat, laden with the community's symbolic sins, out into the desert. In this way, the community discharged its sins and could start afresh. During epidemics, the Hittites used to infect a scapegoat with the disease and send it to the dwelling-place of foreign gods, so that the sickness might be taken away from them.

These symbolic drawings, or pictograms, were painted by the Dogons on rock faces. Their meaning only becomes clear to initiates during the ceremonies which mark the passage to adulthood.

The labyrinth of intestines, according to a Mesopotamian carving. The curling pathways of the intestine formed an image of the universe, and were interpreted by diviners when animals were sacrificed. In a variety of traditions, they were a symbol of order and chaos, of the road to knowledge, of the road leading through the maze to the heart of knowledge.

Esoteric knowledge (from the Greek meaning 'inner') was knowledge given verbally during initiation.

There is an unavoidable fascination with the invisible, the unspoken, the mysterious which lies at the heart of all religions. Some religious traditions are based on that mysterious heart, saying that the truth, hidden from the understanding of the multitude just as a kernel is hidden inside the fruit, must only be revealed to a select group of initiates.

In Greek and Roman times, there were mystery cults dedicated to Isis, Cybele, Dionysus, Demeter... Most religions have one or more secret strands running through them, strands which vary in importance according to the times: in Judaism, the Kabbalah; in Islam, Sufism; in Buddhism and Hinduism, the Tantras.

For these religions, knowledge is reserved to the elect, that is to say, to those who have sought and completed a series of tests, or initiations, in order to receive from the Master the mastery that he himself once earned.

This quest for truth is the bright and luminous side of the fascination of mystery; the dark side is called the occult, or magic. Magic deals with darkness, and is founded in fear. It has an important place in archaic societies or attitudes of mind. The best protection of all against these practices is simply not to believe in them.

Mystery

In antiquity, the mystery religions (from the Greek word, *mustes*, meaning 'initiate') were based on doctrines which were only unfolded to initiates who worked deeper and deeper into the heart of the religion. This was the function of such rituals as the mysteries of Eleusis in Greece, or of Isis in Rome.

Religion is the experience of mystery; it comes about when emotions are open to the eternal reality which we can perceive through the veil of the temporal.
Rudolph Otto

That hidden Being who can be seen everywhere in his creation, it is for Him I long
Rumi, 13th century Muslim mystic

A magic scroll from Ethiopia (about 242 cm by 21 cm) of a demon, painted in the 18th century. These kinds of paintings acted as talismans: they were thought to contain an invisible protective presence which could exorcize illness and exert a healing power.

What is a mystic?

An African mask seeking to represent ideal human beauty.

Carving of a Mesopotamian priest at prayer

We should not round off this brief description of those elements which make up religion without referring to mystical experience, still one of the most vivid and intense of all religious phenomena.

Wherever and whenever they may occur, religions have as their source and their regeneration the meeting which people experience between themselves and the divine, whether as a person or as a thought. Such meetings shape their emotions, their ideas, their actions, their entire existence. It is that emotional relationship which defines mysticism.

As always where feelings are concerned, emotional response precedes rational interpretation. But it is not very long before the human need for order and understanding tries to provide reasons for loving (or fearing) the being who is loved (or feared).

Such an encounter is sometimes accompanied by abnormal phenomena for which there seems to be no rational explanation: levitation (rising bodily into the air), visions, various ecstatic states and trances.

Trances and possession

In animism (the belief that all objects possess souls) and some so-called primitive religions, the religious experience sometimes comes through possession. It is as though some supernatural being borrows the body and mind of the subject, while he or she remains in a trance.

God or man?

Often, people give their gods human characteristics. This alabaster statue from about 3000 BC, found in a megalithic tomb (p. 63) in Spain, is one of the first representations of the human face. It is probably an idol. But mystics devote their energies and thoughts to losing their basic human aspect in an effort to become more and more like their god in spirit.

The Hindu pilgrim Sudama, wandering in search of supreme wisdom, draws close to his goal: the god Krishna's City of Gold. (from an 18th century Indian miniature)

When he goes to the ocean in search of a pearl, he is himself the pearl, perhaps even the only pearl.
> Rumi, 13th century Muslim mystic

But to concentrate on the more spectacular manifestations of mysticism is to risk forgetting the central truth that for the believer, an encounter with his god can be an experience that is just as normal and just as extraordinary as falling in love.

The soul and God delight in each other in the midst of an enormous silence.
> Teresa of Avila, 16th century Christian mystic

Let the Yogi constantly strive for union with the Self... That is the divine union... Then the Yogi will receive – supreme, spotless, without passion – the spiritual bliss which the Brahma has become.
> Bhagavad-Gita VI, Hindu sacred text

A Muslim mystic prays in the hollow tree which symbolizes the knowledge of divine mysteries (16th century Persian miniature)

RELIGIONS OF THE PAST

Prehistory

Old Stone Age

1½ million years ago:
Homo habilis
500,000 years ago:
fire first used
150,000 years ago:
Homo sapiens
70,000 years ago:
earliest burials
40,000 years ago:
Cro-Magnon man;
first bone carvings
30,000 years ago:
carved figurines
25,000 years ago:
first cave paintings
10,000 years ago:
bow and arrow

New Stone Age

9,000 years ago:
earliest domestic
animals
8,000 years ago:
first known city
(Jericho). Cereal
cultivation begins
6,000 years ago:
hunting gives way
to farming (Europe)

Bronze Age

4,800 years ago: ear-
liest megaliths
4,000 years ago:
Egyptian boats ply
the Mediterranean
3,500 years ago:
The wheel
(Sumeria)
Horses tamed
Earliest writing

Female head, 36mm high,
carved from mammoth
tusk about 22,000 years
ago; found in SW France

We can tell from remains left behind that about 80,000 years ago people had begun to think about the afterlife and to fashion objects relating to it: paintings, statuettes, graves and funeral monuments.

Neanderthal people, living 80,000 to 40,000 years ago, had rites for the dead. About forty burial sites have been found in Europe and the Middle East. In one, at Shanidar in Iraq, a child was laid on a bed of flowers. This happened over 50,000 years ago, between May and July, so scientists have gathered from dating the pollen.

People physically similar to us, called Cro-Magnon men, lived in Europe during the last ice ages, about 40,000 to 10,000 years ago. They also placed their dead in graves. Archaeologists have found about eighty of their skeletons.

Art was another of Cro-Magnon man's activities, connected perhaps with the supernatural. Prehistoric paintings and engravings, some as old as 17,000 years, decorate caves in south-west France. The most spectacular are at Lascaux. There are images of powerful bison, galloping horses,

Skeleton from the late Stone Age bearing traces of ochre dye, found in south-west France. The digging of a grave, the red ochre, the offerings placed in it such as bison hooves, stag antlers, beads, flowers, weapons and tools of flint and bone, suggest that there were sacred rites for burials then.

Stone or ivory statuettes, known as Venus figures, show that woman's fertility was revered. This one, about 22,000 years old,

fearsome bears and tigers, as well as mammoths and woolly rhinos: all animals that people were in awe of, or hunted for meat and skins. Human figures are there too: strange witch doctors and hunters in disguise. But it was really the animals, the providers of food and warmth, that dominated their world and their imaginations.

Lascaux cave painting, about 17,500 years old, showing a man being gored by a wounded bison.

is from Austria.

Megalithic culture

Funeral stone from Saint-Sernin in central France; it is a highly stylized statue of a woman with bare breasts and a necklace – a 'mother goddess'. The mystery of fertility obsessed the earliest people who cultivated crops.

Between four and six thousand years ago the earliest farmers erected huge stones called megaliths. They were either placed individually in an upright position or arranged one on top of the other. These formed shrines where people's ancestors were honoured, or the wise men of the earliest settlements were laid to rest.

Hundreds of these stones survive to this day. The oldest and most spectacular of these sacred monuments are in western Europe: Malta, Spain and Portugal, France, the British Isles, northern Germany, and Denmark.

Some of these stones are arranged as a table; this is a 'dolmen'. When covered with stones and earth and ringed by walls it is called a tumulus. Tumuli were used as burial chambers.

A passage made through the tumulus led to the grave. Human bones and offerings such as vases, arrowheads, polished axes and jewellery have been found on such sites.

Reconstruction of a burial chamber found in Britain.

The burial chamber was sometimes decorated with figures of mother goddesses, representing fertility. There were also drawings of polished axes, bows and crooks symbolizing male power. Natural elements – sun, moon, water, wind and earth all seem to have had their own symbols.

Dolmen at Bagneux in western France

At Stonehenge, in Wiltshire (England), giant stones were laid out so that, at the summer solstice, someone standing in the middle would see the rays of the rising sun strike a single free-standing stone on the outskirts. A similar effect was devised at Newgrange in Ireland.

The tall, upright stones, called 'menhirs', are as old as the dolmens. Since they have similar decorative markings, menhirs probably also played a part in the religious ceremonies of the time. The largest menhir was found at Locmariaquer in Brittany. It weighed 350 tonnes.

Awe-inspiring ceremonies must have taken place in this monumental setting in Carnac, Brittany.

Altar found in a burial chamber in Malta, which is rich in megalithic remains.

Mesopotamia

Archaic statue of a god carved in alabaster with lapis lazuli eyes (about 3000 BC)

Priest making an offering of cereals to a deity (from a cylindrical seal, 2000–3000 BC)

The religion of ancient Mesopotamia is one of the oldest of which any traces have been found. It grew and developed for over 3,000 years, perhaps the longest time-scale of any known religion: from about 3,000 BC to about the first century AD.

This religion arose when two completely different civilizations met and mingled in the same place: Semites (later known as Akkadians) came from the north west, and Sumerians from an unknown area in the south east. The Sumerians seem to have been intellectually dominant: it was they who gave names to several of the gods and who contributed most of the religious ritual. But they disappeared about 2500 to 2000 BC, absorbed by the Semites, who were more numerous and vigorous.

The Mesopotamian religion was thus Sumero – Akkadian in origin and in the languages used. In spirit, it was related to the religions of the ancient Semites: Hebrews (p. 136), Canaanites, Phoenicians, Aramaeans and Arabs (p. 80).

Animal figures in glazed brick decorated the walls of the processional route in Babylon when the city was rebuilt by King Nebuchadnezzar II, around 600 BC.

Babylon, the 'Gate of the Gods', was founded 3000 to 4000 BC and had several periods of splendour. Its last golden age was under Nebuchadnezzar II, who built the double walls and the monumental gate of Ishtar, goddess of love, decorated with bas-reliefs. (Reconstruction from the Berlin museum)

Ancient river courses of Mesopotamia are shown in dotted lines.

*Heaven created Earth; Earth created the River;
the River created the Stream,
and the Stream created Mud.*
Babylonian myth (about 2000 BC).

Hero, (Gilgamesh?) wrestling with a lion (cylinder seal, 2000–3000 BC)

Mesopotamia means 'between rivers' in Greek. In the south were marshes, where the reeds were cut to make huts, though brick was also widely used as a building material. The fearsome floods of the Tigris and Euphrates probably gave rise to the myth of Noah's ark.

Sacred writings

Half a million clay tablets, sun-dried or kiln-fired, have been discovered in archaeological excavations. On them, copyists, scribes and writers of the period wrote down what they wanted to remember.

Most of the tablets are everyday official documents (inventories, contracts and judicial records). About a fifth are inscribed with more literary writing, dealing with cultural, intellectual, emotional, moral and religious life. There are treatises on grammar, medicine, mathematics and astrology, technical manuals, as well as literary essays. In particular, there are writings of a religious kind: hymns, prayers, official forms of service, exorcisms and pious legends and myths explaining the actions of the gods, the origins of the world and the purpose of existence.

Head of the stone on which King Hammurabi had 282 legal decisions engraved to show his wisdom as judge and ruler: he made sure that he was shown receiving the emblems of authority from the god, Marduk (*c.* 1760 BC).

The biblical story of the Flood, early in the 1st millennium BC, follows fairly closely a Babylonian myth written at least seven centuries before.

It tells how men, mortal but blessed with long life, so multiplied that their chatter kept the king of the gods awake. By disease at first, then by famine, he tried to make a drastic reduction in their numbers. But the clever god, Ea (or Enki), who created them saved them from this twin danger. So the king of the gods resolved to destroy them by a massive flood, caused by torrential rains; such rain occurs from time to time in the region. So Ea then chose the best man among them and taught him how to make a boat. With his family, land animals of all kinds, and his new technological know-how, he set sail and so escaped death.

Men were then allowed to stay on earth, but their lifespan and fertility were reduced so as to shield them from similar dangers in the future.

The earliest writing appeared in Mesopotamia about 3000 BC.

The earliest signs were pictograms, simplified drawings

made by the imprint on clay of a pointed stylus. Later they were pressed in with a bevelled reed (*calamus*). This was called 'cuneiform' (wedge-shaped) writing, because of the shape of the characters.

67

These bearers of food and drink waited on the gods, whose four daily meals were an essential part of worship.

Temples were not the only places of worship. Near them were stepped towers called 'ziggurats' on top of which were small sanctuaries. These were seen as the stairs used by the god to come down to earth and the means for the faithful to approach him more closely by climbing heavenwards.

Worship and sanctuaries

According to an ancient myth, Ea invented and made mankind to come to the assistance of the gods, who were tired of having to get their own meals. The natural role of human beings was therefore to produce, by their labour, all things necessary to make sure the gods had lavish and carefree lives.

So houses were built for them, magnificent temples with rich furniture and with statues which both represented them and seemed to make them really present. In daily services and on solemn feast days the gods were offered choice food and drink in plenty, served with incense, music, singing and the reciting of myths commemorating their great deeds.

Statues of the gods were taken out, too, on picturesque processions in chariots and boats to meet each other or to pay each other visits in their sanctuaries. Even their marriages were celebrated in strict rotation.

This small bronze plate comes from the 12th century BC and shows a ceremony taking place in front of a temple. The two crouching figures are either carrying out a ritual cleansing, or perhaps are making offerings. They squat beside a small altar and a stone jar containing holy water.

People had to realize that they had certain religious, civil and moral duties. Neglecting them was an act of revolt against their masters – a sin. As punishment, the gods could order demons to inflict misfortune on the guilty. This was the reason for all the evils which plagued their lives. However, acts of worship could persuade the gods to relent.

Ur-Nanshe, King of Lagash about 2500 BC, celebrates the foundation of a temple. Here he is shown on a plaque celebrating his achievements: He is seen as a mason, at work on a temple built to his own glory.

Oh Shamash,
perched on the mountain-top you watch over the Earth,
From Heaven on high you grasp the whole
world in your hands,
Your care is for everyone here below.
Hymn to the sun god, about 2000 BC

Below: Adad, armed with thunderbolts, rides the sky on a young bull, his emblem. Lightning and storm are his to command.

The gods

Mesopotamian religion was made up essentially of fear, admiration and servile respect. Divine beings were addressed as important dignitaries:

Oh Lord! Supreme ruler! On Earth and in Heaven alone great!

Sovereign over the ends of the earth, to exalt thy greatness is my deepest wish!

Thy godhead shines with a glory loftier than Heaven!

And vaster than the sea!

This kind of worship has no place for love, mysticism or a close personal relationship with god. The gods were linked with the natural world, which could be either violent or orderly. Like the storms, epidemics and floods, supernatural beings were beyond human comprehension. They were shown in mankind's image, but more powerful, intelligent, and blessed with everlasting life.

Divine society, too, was seen as being organized along human lines. The ruler at the top was Enlil ('Lord Wind' in Sumerian) and his father An or Anu (Heaven), the founder of the holy family. Enlil was assisted by Ea (or Enki), the most intelligent of the gods.

Other deities, who numbered nearly 2,000, were in charge of every aspect of the universe: sun, moon, rain, storm, crop and animal fertility, and so on.

At the end of the 2nd millennium Enlil abdicated in favour of a younger god, as his own father had done. Marduk, Ea's son, took the throne and held absolute power.

In the middle the Sun, Shamash, leaves his mountain, flanked by Ea, god of the waters, and, it seems, by Ishtar, goddess of love, and Ninurta, god of war.

Ram leaning against a tree. Wooden statuette covered in gold, silver and lapis lazuli, 50 cm in height, found in a tomb at Ur (3rd millennium)

Pazuzu, a demon sent by the angry gods to bring pestilence to mankind.

Why hurry so, Gilgamesh?
You will never attain the everlasting life you seek!
When the gods created mankind
Death they assigned to them
Keeping for themselves life immortal!
Epic of Gilgamesh

Right: King Gudea is led by his patron deity to be presented to a more powerful god.

King bearing a lamb for sacrifice to a god, perhaps as part of daily worship or at a religious festival, such as new year's day – held in spring

Exorcism and divination

The idea was to use prayers and different sorts of magic to eliminate an evil by exorcizing, or expelling, whatever had caused it, especially if it were a demon. For instance, evil was passed on to another object or animal by rubbing, or by prolonged contact. This became the 'scapegoat' that was then cast out or destroyed, by suffocation, drowning, burning, or being torn to pieces.

Many such exorcisms are still remembered, particularly against diseases, even though ordinary medicine was used as well.

Sometimes the gods, on whom everything depended, decided to

plant some unexpected, out-of-the-ordinary happening into daily life. It might be the birth of a monster, a particular dream, or something unusual in the intestines of a sacrificed animal. They did so because they wanted to draw attention to a decision they had taken, concealed but possible to decipher. So an intricate code was worked out to explain strange events. Thus, a stillbirth might herald the early death of one of the parents.

Death had no great significance, it was simply the inevitable fate of mankind. The body, once laid to rest, turned back to the clay which Ea had used to model the original man. There was no judgement day: a kind of shadowy double flitted off to join all the other phantoms in the underworld. There they led a silent, sleepy existence, their modest needs met by small gifts from the living.

So, fill your belly; be joyful day and night. Day and night make merry; put on fine clothes. Wash, bathe; watch tenderly your little one holding your hand. And may the wife of your bosom be happy! For such is the lot of mankind!
Epic of Gilgamesh

Statuettes of worshippers (around 2000 BC)

Clay liver used by soothsayers as a handbook, to read the messages of the gods in the livers of sacrificial animals (1900 BC)

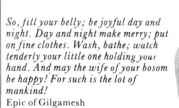

Person at prayer (bronze statuette, 1800 BC)

Ancient Egypt

Cover of an alabaster funeral vase showing the Pharaoh Tutankhamen. His headdress is decorated with vulture and cobra heads, symbolizing sovereignty.

MEDITERRANEAN SEA

LOWER EGYPT

Nile

UPPER EGYPT

RED SEA

An 'Appeal to the Living' was carved on the tomb. Reading it magically enabled food gifts to be renewed and so ensured the dead person's survival. But other spells pronounced terrible curses on desecrators.

The River Nile flows a thousand miles through Egypt from its source in the great central African lakes to a large delta on the Mediterranean, with desert on either side. For nearly 3,000 years the country was ruled by Pharaohs. The Greeks under Alexander the Great conquered it, and then the Romans took it over, exploiting it as a source of grain.

Creeds

The Egyptian religion was based on two vital elements: sun and water. Every day the sun brought life again while the water of the Nile made plants grow by depositing fertile mud on the land during the annual flood.

Villages and the first towns grew up along the valley, and the holy places of numerous gods were established.

From the time of the first pyramids, about 2800 BC, the Egyptians looked to Ra, the sun god, for life itself, and to Hapi, the Nile in flood, for all other benefits. They also prayed to other

Pyramids were the final resting places of the Pharaohs. Worship took place in a funeral temple nearby. At Giza the remains of the temple can still be seen with the sphinx defending the tombs. The pyramids reached heights of 137 m.

74

gods for everyday needs.

Sacred writings

Inscriptions in hieroglyphics (meaning 'sacred signs') describe worship

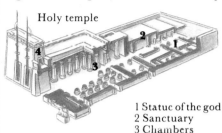

Holy temple

1 Statue of the god
2 Sanctuary
3 Chambers
4 Pylons (gates)

and ritual. How the king survived death is revealed in the 'Pyramid texts'. From 1500 BC, the 'Book of the Dead' advised how every dead person could travel in the beyond. Scribes have left teachings on papyrus scrolls.

Priests and worship

Every Egyptian could entrust the priests with offerings and prayers to secure world harmony and earthly needs. These rites took place in holy temples where the god might reveal himself in oracles that the priests would then interpret.

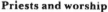

Temple of Isis on the island of Philae

Funeral Cults

Priests were responsible for the cult of the dead. Tombs were grouped together in a 'necropolis' or city of the dead. Services were held on an altar or near a stone.

Funeral complex

1 Pyramid
2 King's chamber
3 High temple
4 Gallery
5 Reception temple
6 Landing stage

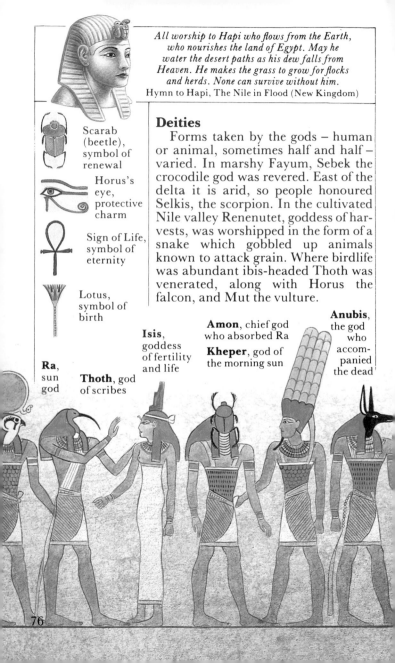

*All worship to Hapi who flows from the Earth,
who nourishes the land of Egypt. May he
water the desert paths as his dew falls from
Heaven. He makes the grass to grow for flocks
and herds. None can survive without him.*

Hymn to Hapi, The Nile in Flood (New Kingdom)

Scarab
(beetle),
symbol of
renewal

Horus's
eye,
protective
charm

Sign of Life,
symbol of
eternity

Lotus,
symbol of
birth

Deities

Forms taken by the gods – human
or animal, sometimes half and half –
varied. In marshy Fayum, Sebek the
crocodile god was revered. East of the
delta it is arid, so people honoured
Selkis, the scorpion. In the cultivated
Nile valley Renenutet, goddess of harvests, was worshipped in the form of a
snake which gobbled up animals
known to attack grain. Where birdlife
was abundant ibis-headed Thoth was
venerated, along with Horus the
falcon, and Mut the vulture.

Ra,
sun
god

Thoth, god
of scribes

Isis,
goddess
of fertility
and life

Amon, chief god
who absorbed Ra

Kheper, god of
the morning sun

Anubis,
the god
who
accom-
panied
the dead

76

Sceptres, symbols of power and prosperity

Pillar, symbol of stability associated with Osiris

Crown of Osiris, lord of the dead

Combined crowns of Upper and Lower Egypt, symbol of power over the whole of Egypt

Nut, the arch of Heaven, is separated from Geb, the Earth, and supported by Shu, the atmosphere. Another myth credits the god Ptah with the creation simply by pronouncing it.

Hathor, cow goddess of heaven and love

Horus, falcon god, son of Isis and Osiris

Osiris, fertility god, judge of the dead

Khnum, the ram, god of the Nile flood

Mayet, goddess of divine order

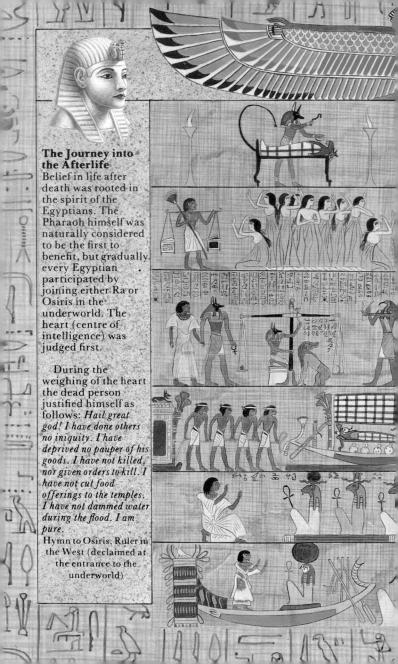

The Journey into the Afterlife

Belief in life after death was rooted in the spirit of the Egyptians. The Pharaoh himself was naturally considered to be the first to benefit, but gradually every Egyptian participated by joining either Ra or Osiris in the underworld. The heart (centre of intelligence) was judged first.

During the weighing of the heart the dead person justified himself as follows: *Hail great god! I have done others no iniquity. I have deprived no pauper of his goods. I have not killed, nor given orders to kill. I have not cut food offerings to the temples. I have not dammed water during the flood. I am pure.*

Hymn to Osiris, Ruler in the West (declaimed at the entrance to the underworld)

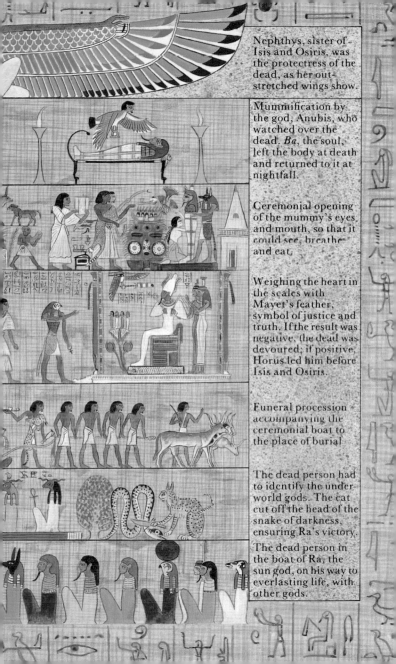

Nephthys, sister of Isis and Osiris, was the protectress of the dead, as her outstretched wings show.

Mummification by the god, Anubis, who watched over the dead. *Ba*, the soul, left the body at death and returned to it at nightfall.

Ceremonial opening of the mummy's eyes and mouth, so that it could see, breathe and eat.

Weighing the heart in the scales with Mayet's feather, symbol of justice and truth. If the result was negative, the dead was devoured; if positive, Horus led him before Isis and Osiris.

Funeral procession accompanying the ceremonial boat to the place of burial

The dead person had to identify the underworld gods. The cat cut off the head of the snake of darkness, ensuring Ra's victory.

The dead person in the boat of Ra, the sun god, on his way to everlasting life, with other gods.

The Semites

Stele (16th century BC) from a temple in Ugarit dedicated to the god of storm. It shows the Lord, Baal, brandishing a thunderbolt.

The Semites are not a race, but a group of peoples descended, according to the Bible, from Sem, one of Noah's three sons.

Emerging about 5,000 years ago from the vast desert of Arabia, the Semites spread throughout the fertile crescent (see map). Eventually they settled, and over the centuries developed brilliant civilizations: the Babylonians in Mesopotamia, and the Canaanites (Phoenicians and Hebrews) on the coast at the eastern end of the Mediterranean. About 1000 BC the Hebrews made Jerusalem the capital of a kingdom worshipping one god. Before long this greatly influenced other religions. A breakaway group of Phoenicians emigrated to North Africa and founded Carthage, soon to become the leading naval power. In the 6th century AD the Arabs founded a new religion, Islam, which recognised the Hebrew prophets of the Bible as forerunners of Muhammad (p. 182).

Bronze censer with zither player (Phoenician cult-object found in Cyprus)

Their beliefs

The ancient Semites were shepherds and traders. Being organized in tribes they had a highly developed sense of the family; although nomadic, and so fairly scattered, they held on to a number of shared customs and beliefs. They revered the god El, a wise old man known as 'The Ancient of Days' or 'The Most High'. He was supported by various deities, the most famous of whom were Baal, the storm god, and Astarte, the goddess of fertility. Semitic rites were simple: they worshipped symbols of divinity in the form of raised stones on hilltops (p. 48) and made regular pilgrimages to holy places. They sacrificed animals (mostly camels and rams) to the god El.

The Semitic peoples form a distinct group to this day. Their languages – Arabic, Ethiopian, Hebrew and Aramaic – have many similarities.

In the 15th century BC, the Canaanites invented alphabetical writing, on which our alphabets are based.

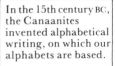

Goddess of fertility

The geographical position of the Phoenicians explains their talent as seafarers. They lived on the narrow strip between Mount Lebanon and the sea.

The fertile crescent (brown arc, *left*) is a well-irrigated area, prosperous in contrast with the arid desert of the Arabian peninsula.

Greek mythology

'Mythology' is a body of myths, sacred stories about the gods and the world, handed down the generations. Myths are not historically true, but can have profound symbolic truth.

About 2000 BC the Greeks came down from the plains further north in Europe and settled the Mediterranean shores of the Balkan peninsula and the islands of the Aegean Sea. They encountered peoples from the East: Phoenicia, Asia Minor and possibly Egypt.

Greek religion did not consist of doctrines or rules that people had to believe to avoid offending the gods. All they had to do was to acknowledge that the gods existed, sacrificing to them according to tradition.

Discus thrower

The Great Games took place every four years in Greece's holy places: at Olympia in honour of Zeus, at Corinth in honour of Poseidon, at Nemea in the Peloponnesus in honour of Hercules, and at Delphi in homage to the serpent, Python, killed by Apollo who adopted its oracle.

GREECE   Troy   ASIA MINOR
Athens
AEGEAN SEA
CRETE

■ Greece
■ Greek colonies

Ancient
Greek theatre

They all had their own gods and forms of worship, as well as their own beliefs.

Greek Literature

Influenced by so many cultures, a form of religion gradually developed, based partly on a mythology inspired by a largely oral tradition. Writings consisted of

– Epic poetry: the most famous epics are the *Iliad* and the *Odyssey*, both attributed to Homer and composed around 800 BC. The *Iliad* describes the war the Greeks waged against the Phrygian city of Troy, and the *Odyssey*, the adventures of Ulysses, a Greek warlord, homeward bound from Troy to the island of Ithaca. The *Theogony* of Hesiod (8th century BC) tells the story of the origins of the universe and the birth of the gods.

– Lyric poetry: Pindar, for instance, celebrated victories at the Olympic Games.

– Tragedies: Aeschylus, Sophocles and Euripides were the main writers of drama (5th century BC).

Writers freely adapted myths. So did artists (vase painters and sculptors) who depicted gods and goddesses in a variety of forms.

In addition, every city had special cults in honour of heroes, each worshipped according to its own customs.
(p.84)

Bards and minstrels travelled from place to place declaiming their poems and playing on the zither.

The Aegean Sea, separating Europe from Asia, takes its name from King Aegeus, the father of Theseus, who fought the Minotaur – the monster, half man and half bull – in Crete. On his return, Theseus forgot to hoist the white sail to signal he was safe. Aegeus, thinking his son dead, threw himself into the sea.

The sphinx was a winged creature with a lion's body and a woman's head.

'Nymph' means young woman. The nymphs represented the female element in nature.

The gods

In the beginning Chaos, the *Yawning Void*, reigned. Then came Earth (herself a goddess), and Eros, love. Chaos had two children: Erebus (the Darkness of Hell) and Night. Earth bore Uranus (the Sky) and the Mountains. Marrying Uranus, she gave birth to Ocean, the Titans (the youngest of which was Cronus), the Cyclops, and to three Giants with a hundred heads and fifty arms. Ashamed of his children, Uranus locked them up. He was mutilated by Cronus, and from his blood sprang deities like Aphrodite (goddess of love). Cronus married his sister, Rhea, and fathered several gods, including Zeus who eventually dethroned him.

Zeus had numerous love affairs which led to the birth of other gods and heroes. From his head came Athena, goddess of reason and protectress of cities.

Every aspect of life was linked with some supernatural being. There were water and tree nymphs, satyrs with goats' legs, centaurs – half men, half horses. Ghosts and witchcraft had their goddess too, named Hecate.

Heroes

Between men and gods were heroes, mortals who by their great deeds had become almost equal to the gods.

Zeus, king of the gods

84

The judgement of Paris: Aphrodite, goddess of love, Eros, Athena, goddess of wisdom, and Hera, wife of Zeus. The shepherd Paris had to choose the most beautiful. His choice of Aphrodite led to the Trojan war.

Demeter, Zeus's sister, goddess of the harvest

Poseidon, Zeus's brother, god of the sea

Asclepius the healer, patron of doctors

Ares, god of war, son of Zeus and Hera

One of the twelve labours of Hercules: the capture of Geryon's herds

Dionysus, god of wine and drama, son of Zeus and Semele

Apollo, god of medicine, poetry and prophecy, and **Artemis**, goddess of the hunt and the moon: children of Zeus and Leto

One of the three Gorgons whose gaze turned people to stone

It is Apollo who cures men and women of their pains, who made a gift of the lyre, and sends the Muse to whom he pleases; he fills hearts with peace and harmony and rules over the oracle's cave.
Pindar, *Pythian Ode V*, 85–92

Rites and Festivals

Public and private life in Greece was dominated by the consultation of oracles – priests or priestesses responding on behalf of a god with often obscure utterances. The most famous was Apollo's shrine at Delphi, where people put questions to the Pythoness, a divinely inspired priestess who gave enigmatic answers in verse form. But there were many other oracles: at Dodona in Epirus, an oak sacred to Zeus 'spoke' through the rustling of its leaves. Seers read signs concealed in animal entrails. Calchas and Tiresias were the best known of these.

The sacrifice of animals was a basic tenet of Greek religion. People usually made offerings to the gods in the form of an animal, and ate it as a form of

The dead were thought to need the bare essentials in the hereafter. So libations – sprinklings of wine or water – were made to them.

The best known Greek religious festival, the Panathenaea of Athens, was celebrated every four years with dancing, feasting and torch-light processions. People filed up to the Acropolis, the hill in Athens where the Parthenon, a temple dedicated to Athena, still stands, and offered the goddess a veil woven by girls – the 'peplo'.

communion when the sacrifice was made to a god above, or burned it when the god was an underworld deity. Wine, honey, wheatmeal and flowers were also given. Every occasion called for specific sacrifices: marriages, journeys, and public holidays. Every city, too, had its own festivals.

As well as worship open to everyone, there were 'mysteries' accessible only to initiates. At Eleusis the carrying off of Persephone by Hades, god of the underworld, and her mother Demeter's search for her across the world, were performed to symbolize the life cycle of the plants and the fate of souls after death.

Calf on the way to sacrifice (after 6th century BC sculpture)

The Hittites

Temples

These resemble Mesopotamian temples: rites and sacrifices took place in a chamber, whilst the sanctuary, to which only the priests had access, housed the statue of the god. Clergy were in charge of daily business in the temples: offerings, purification rites, and the care of the statue. The high priest was the king, acting as intermediary between his people and the gods. At Yazilikaya (13th century BC), 65 deities were carved in the rock. Each held an identifying emblem.

For the storm god, the new year will be celebrated
as a major festival of the sky and the earth.
All the gods are assembled
and going to the house of the storm god.
From a Hittite ritual

The ancestors of the Hittites, the Hattis, occupied the Anatolian plain (today's Turkey). Around 2000 BC, they were invaded by a tribe which intermarried with them and taught them its language. From this racial mixture grew the Hittite empire; in trying to expand its territory it provoked its powerful neighbours and, in 1170 BC, collapsed. But its civilization survived in scattered princedoms in Syria and Palestine.

Bronze solar disc, found in a Hatti tomb; the donkey (centre) is connected with the god Pirva.

Gold statuette of a god (14th century BC)

Monumental gate at Alaja Huyuk (14th century BC), with a carved sphinx, protector of the city

The gods

Mesopotamia had a strong influence on the Hittite religion. The chief gods were the storm god, his consort the sun goddess, and their offspring.

Writings

The Hittites' beliefs made up a rich mythology, which was duly recorded. *Kingship in Heaven*, the tale of the god Kumarbi's adventures in winning back his king-ship after it had been usurped by another god, may have inspired Hesiod's *Theogony* (p. 83).

The Scythians

Their religion had no temples, altars or statues, only the wide open spaces and sky. Covered waggons, pulled by oxen, were their homes.

The Scythian advance

Deity holding a tree of life

For centuries the peoples of the Middle East lived in dread of seeing the wild marauding hordes, mounted on their tough little horses, pouring down from the northern steppes. Attila's Huns or Genghis Khan's Mongols were already encroaching on the southern plains a thousand years before Christ.

The Scythians were similar to tribes such as these; they were the first people to learn how to ride horses. Horses and sheep made up the bulk of their domestic herds. They worshipped the earth, the sun, rivers and winds. But their favourite deity was Tabiti, goddess of fire, who provided light and warmth during the long cold nights on the steppes. They also revered a god of war, whose emblem was a sword.

Ancestor Worship

When one of their people died the Scythians practised complex rituals before interring him in a wooden house buried in the ground. He was laid to rest, together with his wife and servants (who were strangled), horses, weapons, jewellery, food, wine and jars of oil. They believed that life continued after death. These nomads, it seems, imagined the other world as an endless and beautiful steppe.

Manicheism

Mani was born of Persian parents in AD216. For nearly twenty years he lived in a half-Jewish, half-Christian community, the 'Baptisers'. But, convinced that he was the Holy Spirit whom Jesus had promised to send into the world, he severed his links with Jews and Christians, and became the bearer of a 'Revelation', intended to replace all others. Mani was put to death in Persia in AD277, but the religion he founded spread rapidly. Through the oases of central Asia it reached China, where Marco Polo found devotees, called 'Manicheans', in the 13th century. In the west it made its way via the Balkans to the south of France, where the Cathars (p. 256) were the last to bear witness to it in the 13th and 14th centuries.

Priest holding a sacred text (central Asian MS, 8th–9th centuries). Mani set out his doctrines in numerous works.

MANI'S DOCTRINE

According to Mani, the duty of religion is to teach people that they are radiant beings created by God, until the Spirit of Evil imprisons them in the darkness of matter: the body is matter, but the soul is a spark of divine light. So, people must free themselves from the clinging material world they have fallen into if they hope to recover the lost paradise.

Nowadays Manicheism means a world view based on the two opposing principles of good and evil.

The tree of the three divine generations called into being by the Father to conquer evil (Chinese fresco, 9th–10th centuries)

The Slavs

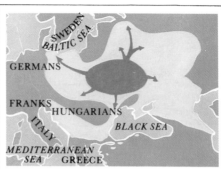

Wood carving of a two-headed deity on a seven-sided pillar (found in East Germany)

The Slavs built many forts which served as princely residences, refuges and store houses. Villages grew up around them.

On Cape Arkona in East Germany a temple was built to the god Svantovit (demolished 12th century).
In its right hand the statue held a horn made of diverse metals that the priest who was initiated in the rites used to fill each year with new wine, in order to bring forth, through the effects of intoxication, the following year's crops.
Saxo Grammaticus
(c. AD 1200)

Slav expansion between the 5th century (in orange) and the 10th century (in yellow)

The Slav people existed as long ago as 2000 BC, but there is no written proof of their religion from that time. Various Slav nations which emerged between the 6th and 10th centuries had no writing until they became Christian. So our knowledge comes either from foreign authors – Latin and Greek – or from Christian Slavs.

In the Soviet Union, Poland and East Germany, archeologists have un-

earthed a few traces of places of worship where sacrifices were made, and stone or wooden sacred images which are difficult to identify.

Nature and ancestor worship

Certain customs lasted a long time, and were connected with two cults. The first expressed mankind's links with nature: special days in the year, like the solstice on 21 June, were celebrated, and the whole of the natural world was peopled with mythical beings. The second dealt with ancestors and their origins; on particular dates they made offerings to the dead and to the deities who watched over births.

The worship of proper gods seems to have arisen quite late and to have caught on only superficially. A thunder god and protector of warriors, called Perin, was honoured in Russia in the 10th century, but other gods are hard to identify; it is not even certain that there were any. But there was an elaborate cult for one called Svantovit on the island of Rügen, East Germany, in the 12th century: offerings were made to him, and his horse issued oracles, which had to be interpreted by priests.

The majority of Slavs had no priests, only witch doctors. They were the only experts on how to cure the sick, and so lingered on in Russia after most people had become Christian.

Lake dwelling

Svantovit, a god with four heads, holding a golden horn in his hand.

The Germanic peoples

Thor, god of war, armed with his magic hammer, does battle with giants and monsters. Giants were a constant threat to the gods (8th century Icelandic MS).

It is mostly thanks to the Roman author, Tacitus, that we know about the beliefs of the Germanic tribes. In the 1st century AD he described some of their methods for foretelling the future, such as observing how horses neighed. Centuries later the Scandinavians, the Germanic people of northern Europe, had kept almost the same religion.

The gods

Odin was the chief god; his power was supreme. To become all-knowing he had given up one of his eyes. Next came Thor, famous for his physical strength. Tyr was the god of justice and victories, Njord of wind and navigation. People prayed to Njord's son Freyr, and his daughter Freyja, for wealth and fertility.

The Germanic world

ICELAND
end of 9th c.
SCANDINAVIA
BRITAIN
end of 9th c.
about 4th c.
GERMANY
Normandy
FRANCE

All the gods made a treaty of friend-ship with each other. One of them, though, the treacherous Loki, brought about the death of the best one among them, the handsome and pure Baldr. Finally, an alliance of giants and monsters resulted in the 'Twilight of the Gods', after terrible natural dis-asters – sun and stars vanishing, flood, earthquake and fire. Most of them were killed, and the reign of the gods associated with Odin came to an end.

Ritual and worship

Worship played a prominent part: during seasonal festivals the Germanic peoples toasted the gods at lavish feasts. Magic rites and prophecy were important too: the runes (a Germanic form of script) enabled people to foil plots against them, to calm storms, to find success in love or cures for illness.

Although most people were Christ-ian by the end of the 11th century some popular traditional customs sur-vived in these Germanic countries.

The **Valkyries** were Odin's messengers. In fantastic rides they came to take part in battles on earth, bringing dead heroes to Odin's palace, Valhalla, and waiting at table during their feasts.

Left hand page: Yggdrasil, tree of the world, is a giant ash. In its branches, which stretch over the whole universe, a learned eagle is perched; stags nibble at its leaves while a serpent gnaws at its roots (17th century Icelandic MS).

Carved stone (8th century) showing the god, **Odin**, on his eight-legged charger, Sleipnir, galloping through the air, and accepting a drinking horn from a Valkyrie; below is a ship of the type the Vikings used.

95

The Celts

Twin-headed Celtic deity (stone sculpture found near Marseilles). One face is turned towards the living, the other towards the dead.

The map shows the Celtic world: in the 7th and 6th centuries BC (yellow); and in the era of its greatest expansion, 3rd century BC (brown).

BRITISH ISLES

GAUL

BALKANS

ASIA MINOR

IBERIAN PENINSULA

The Celts spread from central Europe between 2000 and 1000 BC and continued until the 3rd century BC. Their territory took in Gaul, then the Iberian peninsula, Asia Minor and the British Isles. In remoter islands, Celtic traditions have survived till today.

Men wore a necklace, or torque, which may have had a social as well as a religious significance.

In the 6th century BC Celtic warrior princes were buried in their chariots with the insignia of their rank, furniture, clothing, weapons and pottery.

Tombs were covered with a funeral mound, or tumulus, sometimes with a statue on top.

Worship

What we know of the Celtic religion comes chiefly through the form it took in Ireland. There it was dominated by hero-gods, superhuman beings who, after their time on earth, went to dwell among the dead. Wave after wave of invaders settled in Ireland and were later venerated in ancestor worship. Hero-gods even became part of family and clan family trees; in this way people felt related and united.

Forts built on hilltops, such as Tara, were their refuges and tombs. Scattered tribes assembled there on feast days.

Celtic religion originally involved human sacrifice, the aim being to make the earth fertile. As time passed this practice became less important. Belief in the magic powers of incantations and spells, and the preaching of druids and poets grew, instead. The wizard Merlin belonged to this second tradition.

Giant horse (109 m long) carved into the chalk Downs in Berkshire (possibly 1st century BC)

Monster gripping a human arm in its jaws (limestone sculpture, 3rd century BC)

Statuettes of pilgrims found at the source of the Seine, a holy place where healing goddess Sequana was worshipped

I swear by the god my tribe swears by;
else let the heavens fall in,
the sea overflow
or the earth open up beneath our feet.
Celtic prince's, or hero's, oath

Festivals

Samhain (1 November) marked the new year and the start of the dark season, blurring the boundaries between the world of the

Deities

Lug, the supreme god, gave his name to the city of Lyons (*Lugdunum* in Latin). The Gaulish **Taranis** (Dagda in Ireland), was the god of the spiritual world. **Ogmios** (Irish, Ogma), whose face smiled to the right and glowered to the left, was the god of warrior-might and kingship.

living and that of the dead. On 1 August *Lugnasad* celebrated the light at its zenith.

Cult chariot showing the sacrifice of a stag to a goddess of fertility (7th cent. BC)

Beltana, the festival of fire growing hotter, was held on 1 May and heralded the start of summer. Cattle were driven through the smoke of purifying fires the night before to make them healthy and fertile.

An oral tradition

Druids were found in nearly all Celtic countries; they travelled widely, preserving a sense of unity between the groups. As priests, wise men and seers they kept alive learning and morality. The oak tree was sacred to them and mistletoe that grew on it was gathered during services. Their teaching was entirely oral, a great many texts being learned by heart. A long

The wild boar stood for spiritual authority in Celtic mythology and was often linked with the druids. In Gaul, the hunting and killing of the boar symbolized the mortal running the spiritual to ground.

Gaulish poem which has come down to us, *The Battle of the Thickets*, is one of these. It expresses the Celts' belief in the immortality of the soul and praises the harmony which can exist between human beings. For the Celts death was merely the passage from one world to the next. Exchanges took place continually between the dead and the living.

Cernunos, the Antlered, god of fertility and plenty, and the untamed forces of nature (1st century BC engraving on a silver bowl)

*I have been a wanderer
    in the air,
I have watched the stars,
I have been a word
    amidst the letters,
I have been a book
    from the beginning,
I have been a lamp
    shining
For a year and a half,
I have been a bridge
    over sixty estuaries,
I have been a road,
I have been an eagle,
I have been a coracle*
    adrift on the sea,
I have been the froth
    on the beer.*

from The Battle of
the Thickets

*light, round, wicker boat

99

The Etruscans

Maenad, servant of the Greek Dionysus (Roman Bacchus), carved in the 5th century BC as a temple roof-fixture

ADRIATIC SEA

Arezzo
Tarquinii
Veii
Rome
Tiber

TYRRHENIAN SEA

What we know of this people is found in the area now called Tuscany. Etruria rivalled Rome for the domination of Italy in the 8th to 5th centuries BC.

Did the Etruscans come from the east, from north Europe, or were they a native Italian people? No one knows. Their religion has not yet yielded all its secrets. It was a mixture of ancient beliefs and of oriental, Italian and Greek influences.

Gods

There was a multitude of gods. At the top reigned Tinia, Uni and Menerva, forerunners of the Roman Jupiter, Juno and Minerva. Tinia was very like Jupiter, except that he shared with other gods the privilege of hurling thunderbolts. Artoumes was the Etruscan name of Artemis, the Greek huntress, the Roman Diana. Turan (Venus) means 'mistress', the mother-goddess of the Mediterranean lands.

Contact with Greek sailors and traders changed these local gods. Hell was the realm of Aita (the Greek Hades) and of his wife Phersipnai (Persephone). The infernal pair ruled over a multitude of demons: Charun,

Etruscan bronze of a chimaera, a monster with a lion's body, a serpent for a tail, and the head of a goat on its back

> *A peasant was ploughing his field when he saw rising from the furrow a*
> *white-haired child called Tages who introduced himself*
> *as an envoy from the gods and taught him augury.*
> Etruscan legend, retold by Cicero

one of them, had horses' ears and a hooked nose, and felled his victims with a mallet.

A seer inspects a sacrificial animal's liver; an expert at reading signs, he interprets the gods' will (mirror back, 4th century BC).

Between two shepherds Tages' head emerges from the ground to reveal the source of divine wisdom (stone carving, 2nd century BC).

This Aplu (Roman Apollo) decorated a temple roof at Veii (6th century BC).

Tuchulcha had a greenish complexion and a head covered with snakes; his job was to tell mortals what torments awaited them in hell.

Sacred writings

In the *Etrusca Disciplina* was written the lore on how to interpret the will of the gods. It included the *Book of the Haruspices*, or the art of reading the entrails of animals, the *Book of Thunderbolts*, which gave the meaning of lightning and thunderclaps, and the *Book of Ritual*. None of these texts has survived.

Worship

People did not take part in ceremonies or pray together. Instead, the seer practised mysterious rites on his own. He was a powerful figure, often counsellor to kings. Even the Roman emperors never went anywhere without an Etruscan seer.

The Etruscans believed in the soul's survival. This had a twin aspect. The dead person came back to life in a grave filled with everything needed: furniture, kitchen utensils, weapons; at the same time, there was an imprecise 'after-world' where banquets and games took place, just as on earth. Some frescoes depict the soul's last journey to the under-world under the guidance of winged spirits.

Since their inscriptions have not been deciphered, the paintings which decorate the walls of the tombs are the most reliable source we have for the lives and beliefs of this mysterious people.

The tomb of the Leopards at Tarquinii, shown here, dates from 470 BC and is decorated with banqueting scenes. The egg being held up by a guest was a symbol of immortality.

The afterlife

According to the Etruscans, there were mysterious, divine laws ruling the world, and people had to submit to them. The will of the gods was expressed in nature, but only the haruspice, the soothsayer, knew how to interpret it. Sometimes he was able to ward off ill fate through magic practices and animal – or even human – sacrifices.

Funerary portrait of a couple (terracotta figures on a sarcophagus, 6th century BC)

As the centuries passed, fate weighed increasingly heavily on the Etruscans. Their vision of the afterlife changed after the 4th century BC from an idyll of never-ending parties to a sombre vision of a dismal underworld. No one, however good or bad, could escape it. This coincided with their being attacked and invaded by the Gauls and Romans, marking their final decline.

The Romans

Romulus and Remus, the founders of Rome, were suckled by a she-wolf on the Palatine Hill.

Temples

These were dedicated to a god. Ceremonies took place outside. Public meetings could be held inside.

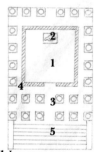

1 Inner room
2 Statue of the god
3 Entrance hall
4 Colonnades
5 Entrance steps

The Romans were soldiers and rulers. Rome began as a small village and within a few centuries had become the capital of a vast empire. Their practical, materialist spirit strongly influenced their religion.

Beliefs

The gods were constantly appealed to over every aspect of daily life. Behind every single thing, every element in nature, the Romans perceived the hand of the gods. River water was a god. A goddess made the flowers grow in springtime. You needed only to refer to a deity to influence the course of events in your favour. So the Romans were alert to anything that could reveal the gods' will to them.

Public and religious business was conducted in the forum. Processions and military triumphs took the Sacred Way.

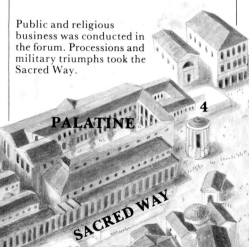

PALATINE

SACRED WAY

Using a crooked staff or *lituus* the soothsayer drew an area on the ground or in the air and in it read divine messages or omens. He interpreted the way birds flew or how the sacred hens, reared just for this purpose, took their food.

The priests

The grand pontiff appointed the seven vestals, virgins dedicated to the worship of Vesta, and the fifteen 'flames', priests attached to a particular god's service. The augurs, soothsayers and *decemvirs* specialized in interpreting omens.

The soothsayer was consulted before any function.

In the 3rd c. BC
In the 2nd c. AD

The Roman empire

1 Temple of Jupiter
2 Temple of Juno
3 Temple of Saturn
4 Temple of Vesta
5 Temple of Concord

CAPITOL

FORUM

The city, too, had gods to protect it.

Jupiter, Juno and Minerva (above) watched over the city of Rome from their temple on the Capitol.

The augurs sacrificed an animal and deciphered its entrails to find out the will of the gods.

The gods

They were numerous and present everywhere: the Lares protected the family; the Penates watched over the larder and the well-being of the home.

Outside the domestic sphere, Faunus ruled over forests and uncultivated land. With him everything was chaos, excess and wild desire. He was worshipped at the Lupercalia, held on 15 February to celebrate the end of winter. Then, people really enjoyed themselves as they do today at carnival time.

Saturn was Father Time, Mercury was connected with trade, Mars was the warrior, Apollo created music and light, Vulcan was the lord of fire, and Neptune the god of the sea. As for

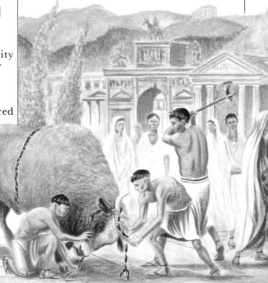

goddesses, Ceres watched over harvests, Diana protected animals and the hunt, Venus dispensed love and victory, and Vesta presided over the home. In the 1st century BC, the emperor was deified and worshipped as well.

The Roman gods increasingly fell under Greek and oriental influences. Mystery cults (p. 54) were very popular, like those of Cybele, mother-goddess of Anatolia, Mithras (p. 239) and Isis (p. 67). The idea of resurrection first emerged in these cults early in the 1st century AD, before Christianity.

Objects used for worship and sacrifice

Ritual and worship

Every house had a domestic altar, the *lararium*, where the *lares* (household gods) were worshipped. The head of the family, who led the prayers, was often portrayed there with two protective spirits.

One of the rites most often practised was the *votum*, the solemn oath to make an offering to a god who granted a particular request. Every general did this before a battle.

Janus is the god both of beginnings (morning, the new year) and of passage (thresholds, city gates).

107

Pre-Columbian civilizations

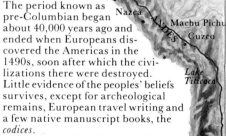

Chichen Itza
• Tikal
Tula
Teotihuacan   Monte Alban
Tenochtitlán   Palenque

— Maya empire
(AD 250–900)
Aztec empire
(AD 1325–1521)
— Inca empire
(AD 1200–1530)   **Pre-Columbian civilizations**

Nazca
Machu Pichu
Cuzco
Lake Titicaca

Machu Pichu, 2000 m up in the Andes, is one of the most remarkable Inca sites.

The period known as pre-Columbian began about 40,000 years ago and ended when Europeans discovered the Americas in the 1490s, soon after which the civilizations there were destroyed. Little evidence of the peoples' beliefs survives, except for archeological remains, European travel writing and a few native manuscript books, the *codices*.

The Spaniards who arrived in the 15th and 16th centuries were astounded to discover highly developed civilizations in the Andean region (from Columbia to central Chile), and Central America (Mexico, Guatemala, Belize, El Salvador, western Honduras, Nicaragua and Costa Rica). The best known were the Aztecs and Mayas in Central America and the Incas in the Andes.

Myths

Pre-Columbian mythology was very rich. An Inca myth tells how a couple emerged from Lake Titicaca and were sent into the region of Cuzco by their father, the sun god, Inti, to bring civilization to mankind. Cuzco city was founded on the spot where the golden wand given them by the sun was driven into the ground. This led to the dynasty of the first rulers.

The Aztec myths tell of the creation of the fifth sun. After being destroyed, together with humanity, four times, it was saved by the sacrifice of the gods who threw themselves in the fire to secure its resurrection.

The sacrifice had to be repeated indefinitely so that mankind would not be annihilated yet again.

The Aztec capital Tenochtitlán, built in 1325 around a ceremonial complex.

Aztec divinatory calendar

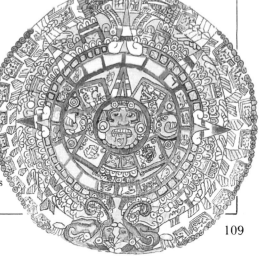

Aztec calendar with the Sun Tonatiuh in the centre.
The Mayas and Aztecs had a solar calendar of 350 days and a religious one of 260 days.

109

He was born, the Maize god,
In the garden of rain and mist,
Where the children of men are created,
Where jade fish are caught.
Aztec song

The gods

The gods gave shape to the forces of nature. Some were anthropomorphic, having human forms, some zoomorphic (animal forms), some combined features from several animals.

Quetzalcoatl, chief god of the Aztecs, also known as the Plumed Serpent

The sun god (Inca silverware)

The Aztecs and Incas were empire-builders long before they themselves were conquered.

Jaguar-god, half-man, half-cat, worshipped by the Olmecs, who occupied Mexico (1200 BC)

The two faces of this statuette represent Death and the Sun. It is of Xolotl, who was similar to Quetzalcoatl, the incarnation of the evening star, Venus. He descended into hell and

Maya god of death

brought back bones to make into people.

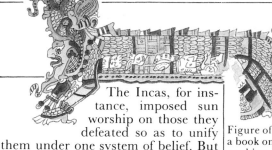

The Incas, for instance, imposed sun worship on those they defeated so as to unify them under one system of belief. But they also acknowledged the local gods of their new subjects. As for the Aztecs, they took over gods from a number of different religions, such as the countryside gods of the native rural peoples.

Figure of a god in a book on astrology, a subject Maya priests brought to a high point of development

Quetzalcoatl originated near the coast where the state of Veracruz now is. He was the god of vegetation and renewal. For the Aztecs he became the god of priests, art and religious thought. He is shown below in the company of Xipe Totec, the vegetation god.

Tlaloc, rain and fertility god, sowing seeds (Teotihuacan fresco)

The god Xochipilli symbolized beauty, love and flowers for the Aztecs.

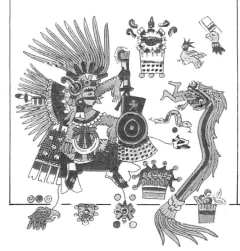

Temples

Cutaway reconstruction of the great Aztec temple at Tenochtitlán. It was rebuilt seven times while the Aztec empire was expanding.

Below: Maya ceremonial complex (Tikal, Guatemala)

Generally, only priests and state dignitaries were allowed into the temple. Public ceremonies were held outside. A typical form of religious architecture was the pyramid, found all over the region but especially on the northern coast of Peru where the Mohicas erected imposing pyramid-shaped platforms between 200 and 700.

In the Maya cities of the classical period (250–900), religious structures became even more colossal, with temples rising 40, 50 or even 72 metres above the ground. The pyramidal

design was intended to serve as a gigantic plinth, raising the sanctuary closer to heaven. It could also serve as a tomb, as in the Pyramid of Inscriptions at Palenque in Mexico, where a crypt was discovered in 1952.

A different kind of structure, something to do with cultural ceremonies, was the ball-game court constructed in Mexico at the time of the Olmecs (from 1150 BC to early 1st century AD).

Facade of the temple of Quetzalcoatl at Teotihuacan

Temple at Chichen Itza (10th–12th centuries). On the right is a sculpture with a hollow belly, which was probably used to hold offerings.

Lord, the precious stone water has rained down.
The tall cypress has been covered with quetzal feathers,
The fire serpent has become the plumed serpent,
So delivering us from the fire serpent.
Hymn to the god Xipe Totec

For these peoples the universe was destroyed and recreated in cycles.

Ritual sacrificial knife or *tumi*, of gold and turquoise, showing the Chimu civilizing hero (north coast of Peru)

Maya funeral mask made of ophite encrusted with coral, turquoise and mother-of-pearl

Rituals and festivals

People worshipped the gods on their own, in families, or in public, in order to induce them to be kind, to persuade them to intervene over something, or to calm their anger. The most common ritual practices were prayers, games, libations (drink-offerings),

combats, offerings and sacrifices.

The Aztecs practised human sacrifice of men, women or children far more than other Amerindian societies. It was the supreme offering, and it alone could fend off the destruction of the world. In peacetime the Aztecs engaged in 'floral war' in which they pitted themselves against allied tribes in order to take prisoners for use in sacrifices.

The Aztecs practised ritual cannibalism.

The Mayas indulged in self-sacrifice too – that is, mutilation or bleeding inflicted on their own bodies during worship.

The Incas held huge religious ceremonies to mark such events as solstices, high points of the farming year, or the coming to power of a new sovereign.

The great temple with twin upper temples, in the Aztec capital, Tenochtitlan

A 9th century fresco decorating a room in a Maya temple at Bonampak, showing a battle and a victory celebration

Volador (Totanac ceremony): the men spin in the air held by their ankles.

The Yucatan Indians, now converted to Christianity, celebrate saints' days with kites similar to the solar discs of their Maya ancestors.

LIVING
RELIGIONS

THE ORAL TRADITIONS

117

Africa

Zaïrean monkey-fetish (monkey with magic powers) carrying a magic bag

Shango, god of thunder and storm, is worshipped by Yoruba smiths and farmers.

Oral traditions

Traditional African religions have no sacred books, so we have to look at what has been passed down by word of mouth from generation to generation. Despite some common features, African beliefs vary widely depending on the individual tribe. A tribe is a group of people with the same language and culture.

Nature religions

In Africa people believe in the presence of mysterious forces in nature. Theirs are 'animist' religions (p. 119). The Ashanti in Ghana, Togo, and the Ivory Coast give the name 'sasa-animals' to those possessing special powers, such as the spider.

. These forces may be revealed in such unusual events as the birth of

Dogon medicine-man sitting in front of a sanctuary (Mali)

twins or a sudden wind. Things have a soul and are inhabited by forces. Either people resign themselves to this and live in fear or they try to win favour through acts of worship.

Oshun, river goddess, is worshipped in Nigeria among the Yoruba.

River, I beg thee to let me catch fish as our ancestors did before me.
Lobi prayer

Ancestors and their afterlife

Belief in the afterlife is widespread. Human beings are often seen as having three elements: a body, a perishable soul and an imperishable one. Ancestors' spirits live among the people for better or for worse, and are worshipped through objects symbolizing them: the central pillar of the hut in the case of the Bambara of Mali, a tiny altar or a smoke-blackened seat with other tribes.

In Madagascar the Malagasy plant zebu horns on their graves, and carve posts with scenes from the dead persons' lives.

Many peoples with an oral religious tradition are 'animists': they believe that every-thing possesses a soul, and that nature is peopled with spirits good or bad.

In the Sudan, a Nuba youth stands guard to prevent the dead person coming back; his body is painted with kaolin, white being the colour of death.

So-and-so came to see me and said he'd eaten (or killed)
*our n'tana. Any wound he gets will be because of the
n'tana he's eaten* (or killed). *Let him be cured
of any illness he suffers from.*
Bambara prayer to appease the sacred animal

[Map showing Areas of animists with labels: Bambara, Bobo, Dogon, Mossi, Lobi, Nuba, Ashanti, Yoruba, Pygmies, Masai, Zulus, Malagasy]

▦ Areas
of animists

Dogon witch-doctors
write in squares the
questions their
clients ask. Markings
left by the desert fox
at night are then
interpreted as
responses from the
Great God.

In June, the Bobo of
Burkina Faso and the
Dogon cover them-
selves with leaves to
celebrate the rains
and seed time.

Spirits

These are not the same as gods or
ancestors. They live everywhere: in
the sky, the stars, on the earth and
under it. People are often afraid of
them because of this.

The desert fox is the oracle of the Dogon
supreme god and shows his will.

The gods

They enjoy superhuman strength
and absolute authority in their own
territory. They often adopt human
shape. In the eyes of many people,
stars are gods.

Many tribes have a 'great god' who
has won a heroic victory over the other
gods. He lives in heaven, far from
people, has no contact with them, and
is hardly worshipped. It was he who
created the world and is the source of
moral law. He is all-seeing, all-
knowing and generally benevolent,
but he can be both kind and cruel at
the same time.

120

Ritual

In African religions rituals are used on countless different occasions. They make generous offerings of the first crops harvested – millet or cotton. They sacrifice animals, such as chicks, hens, sheep or bulls in order to thank or to calm angry gods, or indeed to gain new strength or to become well.

The chief ceremonies are initiation rites, a series of trials undergone by adolescents on the threshold of adult life, or funerals, which are celebrated at great length and expense.

Traditional African religions were deeply rooted in society. They now face fierce competition from Christianity and Islam, and are strongly influenced by both.

Dogon masks

The great Mossi

masks in Burkina Faso make people aware of the presence of invisible forces in everyday life. This one shows a deity on an antelope's head.

Kenyan and Tanzanian Masai (left) celebrating the rite of passage from young warrior status to adult life. The red ochre colour of war is replaced by the white stripes of peace.

121

The South Seas

Statuette set to guard houses from evil spirits (Easter Island)

The colossal statues of Easter Island in Polynesia are carved in volcanic tufa. This material is too fragile to be carved into small shapes.

Their eyes were made of white coral.

Priests are a special caste in eastern Polynesia (from Hawaii to New Zealand). From the age of eight they learn by heart, in special schools, the traditional account of the origin and the activities of the gods. This is not written down, but sung.

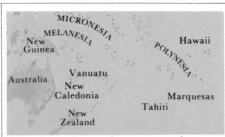

The island peoples scattered across this huge area have handed down their myths by word of mouth. They try to explain the origins of mankind and of civilization.

Gods

The best known and most fully developed myth-cycles are those of the New Zealand Maoris. In the beginning was Te Pu, the void who created Te More because he was tired of the silence. To liven things up he split into two. Still bored, he created the first couple, Night and Death, who were hostile to the world of light; then he made a second couple, Earth and Sky,

who lived close together. Their children needed more space for themselves so Tane, the eldest, managed to separate his parents by taking the form of a cleft tree.

Tane is a god of human beings and of everything that rises towards heaven, such as trees and birds. Mankind, descended from him, is sometimes in conflict with his brothers, the gods of the sea, war, or winds, and sometimes under their protection.

Maui is the hero who brings mankind what it most needs, laying a trap for his grandfather, the sun, to make him slow down and allow day and night to alternate. He also steals fire from his grandmother, the daughter of lightning, asking her for each of her burning fingers in turn. He hides them in the trunks of hardwood trees which people can then rub to make fire.

Houses of the Spirits (Papua New Guinea)

New Guinea warrior dressed for ritual dancing

Rituals

These are usually performed in secret. Fertility rites are the most spectacular. In Tahiti, Hawaii and the Marquesas Islands they take place in houses open to the sky. Many ceremonies are accompanied by dancing for which people paint their bodies and faces, like the Aboriginals shown here. The Flinders Range in S. Australia is one of their sacred sites.

I make my fire burn, whose fire?
Maui's fire, Maui Tikitiki, born of Taranga.
Burnt by what? Burnt by fire.
Whose fire? Mahuika's fire.
Make him get better, so that he may feed us.
Maori spell

The country of the dead is reached by following the roots of a banyan or croton tree. Or else its boundary is the exact spot where a bird with a distinctive call mounts guard.

The South Sea peoples believe that life and death are complementary forms of existence, one balancing the other. While alive, men and women possess technological powers, physical strength and the ability to hand on life. When dead they have powers over nature. To gain this power many people commit suicide believing they will be more able to wreak revenge for a wrong they have suffered.

The dead live far away, in their own country – not an easy one for living people to reach – under the land or the sea, in the crater of an active or extinct volcano, or in a cave. It can even be on an island which starts moving as the living draw near, and on which no European has ever been able to land.

Life, it is thought, is a kind of electric current connecting the generations; the thing people most dread is a break in this current through any failure to produce male children.

The dead

The dead are believed to enjoy a varied life, thanks to their powers. Living on the edge of inhabited and cultivated land they are prayed to when anyone is sick. The ghost of a dead person met on the road heralds a

death in a distant branch of the family. People address the dead directly, without the intercession of a priest, at every emotional crisis.

To reach their own country, the dead follow a path at the cliff edge, or along a ridge in the case of mountainous islands; that way, they cannot cut off a spring or a water-course, symbols of life. Once there they lead a social life similar to that of the living. Taking human shape by day, they revert to a pile of bones at night.

The dead also possess useful knowledge. Following prophetic dreams, proposals for some community action or important reforms are put forward in the name of someone who has died.

Fish ridden by gods (New Ireland carving)

Using the jaw of his grandfather, the sun, as a fish-hook, Maui hauled New Zealand (Ika a Maui) and the surrounding islands from the depths of the sea.

125

The Native Americans

A Sioux at prayer, his sacred pipe pointing skywards

Bowl shaped like a beaver, an animal symbolizing abundance

Nature and mankind were born through the will of the Trickster. In the shape of a crow, rabbit or coyote, he roamed the world with his intestines rolled around his body and a prodigious penis. He did as much mischief as good. He cut open people's hands to make fingers and pierced a hole in their faces to enable them to talk. He invented suffering and tears, and then laughter. He created mountains to make life difficult, but also gave intelligence, strength and courage, and taught magic.

In the early 17th century the first Europeans pushed into the territory of the Indian people on the east coast of North America. When white missionaries tried to convert them, they found that they were deeply attached to their own religious customs.

A Religion of Nature

The Indian is an 'animist': for him, every element in nature is a living thing endowed with a good or evil spirit. Life consists of persuading these spirits to be on one's side, respecting them, and turning aside evil forces. A supreme spirit dominates the universe, but does not intervene much here below. He is

Each clan is under the protection of an animal whose descendants they claim to be. 'Totem' comes from *ototeman*, 'he is a relation'. It unites the clan who worship it.

called *wakan* by the Sioux and *manitou* by the Iroquois. He appears in the wind that ripples over the lake or in the rumble of thunder over the plain.

The Indian must respect the customs of the tribe: any wrong-doing results in illness, the flight of game or bad crops. Prey must be taken with the consent of the 'Master of animals', a mythical beast which watches over its own species. The beaver, for example, must be cut up in a certain way and its bones kept from the dogs.

Bison hunt (top), and rocks piled up to attract them (after Bodmer, 19th century). The bison was the staple food of the Indians of the Plains.

Girls do not follow the same path as boys. Puberty brings magic powers, particularly that of giving birth.

Mask known as 'the speaker's' worn by the Iroquois to fend off evil spirits

Mandan bison dance: the dancer identifies with the bison by wearing its pelt, and in so doing harnesses its strength, too.

The Guardian Spirit

Faced with a host of spirits, the Indian needs to be protected. That is the job of his guardian spirit, whom he sets off to seek when approaching manhood. He must live by himself in the forest,

At the beginning of summer the 'sun dance' takes place to thank the Great Spirit for plants and animals, and it serves to confirm the manliness of the young braves. A tree is planted, around which the dancers turn, watching the sun. They hang from a pole by leather thongs, with bone pins hooked into their skin. As the ceremony proceeds the skin tears and frees the youths, who have thus offered up their suffering to the Great Spirit (from a painting by Catlin, 19th century).

fasting and smoking. After several days' hardship the young man sees the spirit revealing itself in animal or semi-human form. It teaches him magic words and songs, such as the 'Song of Death'. This is what the braves intone in moments of danger. It discloses the contents of the 'medicine bag', the visible token of their alliance, in which the Indian hides sacred objects, always keeping it about him.

The Medicine Man

The guardian spirit may grant supernatural powers – of seeing the future, taming spirits and travelling in the country of the dead. The Indian who has mastered these skills becomes a shaman or medicine man, a specialist in speaking to the supernatural world, healing the sick and chasing away evil spirits.

Principal tribes

The *Katchinas*, companions of ancestors, played here by masked dancers, threaten naughty children.

The bird of storms, an eagle, which causes thunder by beating its wings and letting off lightning with its beak

After death the soul passes through the Milky Way en route to the 'Happy Hunting Grounds', a replica of the world of the living, but where all is pleasure and abundance.

129

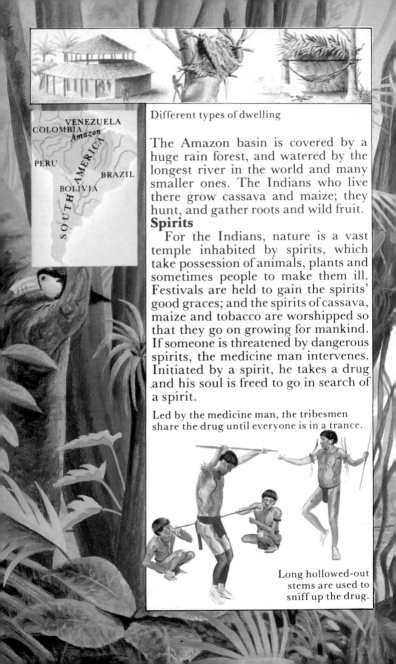

Different types of dwelling

The Amazon basin is covered by a huge rain forest, and watered by the longest river in the world and many smaller ones. The Indians who live there grow cassava and maize; they hunt, and gather roots and wild fruit.

Spirits

For the Indians, nature is a vast temple inhabited by spirits, which take possession of animals, plants and sometimes people to make them ill. Festivals are held to gain the spirits' good graces; and the spirits of cassava, maize and tobacco are worshipped so that they go on growing for mankind. If someone is threatened by dangerous spirits, the medicine man intervenes. Initiated by a spirit, he takes a drug and his soul is freed to go in search of a spirit.

Led by the medicine man, the tribesmen share the drug until everyone is in a trance.

Long hollowed-out stems are used to sniff up the drug.

The Amazonian Indians

Rituals

These mark the stages in life and acceptance into the group. At birth babies are given names to protect them; at puberty a boy is tattooed and tested very harshly to prove his courage. Through marriage he can seek an alliance with another clan. After death, the body is cremated. Some months later, another ceremony frees the living from the presence of the soul which hangs around the village. Singing, dancing and weeping chase it up to heaven. Masks play an important part; under them, the spirit comes alive, makes itself known to the tribe and converses with it.

Feather head-dress worn at initiation rites. The feathers represent the sun.

The necklace of jaguar claws protects the wearer from the animal's magic powers.

Some tribes have their lower lips stretched.

Arctic peoples

Inuit mask showing
the woman in the
moon

Living things – and
stones and trees are
living – possess a
body, a soul, and a
shadow. The woods
and frozen tundra are
populated with
spirits whom only the
medicine-man can
approach.

Anky-Kiele, spirit of
the sea. A medicine
man's spirit goes
down to ask it to send
mankind fish and sea
creatures (from
a drawing by
Tchuktche Onno,
East Siberia, 1945).

The Arctic peoples live in a very
severe climate. Their economy is based
on hunting, fishing and, in some cases,
reindeer farming.

A religion of nature

Most believe that earth was taken,
after a flood, from the bottom of the
original ocean. Our world was created
with part of that earth. It is flat, and a
giant animal holds it up; the sky rests
on pillars, and the vault of heaven
revolves around the pole star. So there
are several worlds, stacked above and
below ours. After death the soul goes
underground to the kingdom of shades.

Rituals

Man is only an element in nature,
not its master. Rites preserve harmony
between creatures. The hunter prays
to the soul of the animal he has killed
so that it tells others that it has been
well treated. In Alaska the harpooned
whale is the *guest* of the village to which
it *gives* its flesh.

GREENLAND
ALASKA
CANADA
SCANDINAVIA
SIBERIA
Hokkaido

The Arctic peoples consist of the Lapps in northern Europe; the Samoyeds and Tungus in Soviet Siberia; the Ainus on the Japanese island of Hokkaido; and the Inuits, in Alaska and Canada.

The bear is a creature held in great respect, as it is among the Indians in North America.

It is considered as being close to human beings. Here the Ainus of Japan sacrifice a cub so that its spirit may beg the gods to make game plentiful.

Grant me to fend off black spirits; give me the strength of a thousand winds to sweep evil aside.
Inuit spell

Gods

All believe in a supreme god: it might be a god of forests and game, a god of thunder, sky and the sun, or a goddess of the sea.

During his trance the soul of the medicine man travels to the land of the spirits, discovers the future, the causes of illness, and how to recover lost game.

133

LIVING
RELIGIONS

THE WRITTEN TRADITIONS

Judaism

The *menorah* or seven-branched candlestick, made to a design given by Yahweh to Moses, has become the emblem of Judaism.

Abraham's journey

MESOPOTAMIA
CANAAN
Hebron
Ur

The birth of a people

The history of the Jewish people began nearly 4,000 years ago at Ur in Mesopotamia (p. 64). Various Semitic peoples (p. 80), including the Hebrews, lived there but were on the move for much of the time. One tribe ventured further than the others: led by Abraham, the Hebrews left Mesopotamia and settled in Canaan. But they were later driven by famine to Egypt, which was rich in grain.

There, the Hebrews gradually fell into slavery, lasting for four centuries (1600–1200 BC). Kept isolated from the Egyptians, they became a closely-knit community, longing to return to Canaan, land of their forefather Abraham. Stories were passed on about their great ancestors such as Isaac and Jacob.

At first the Hebrews were more settled than nomadic. They established themselves in Mesopotamia as herdsmen and farmers.

*Get thee out of thy country, and from thy kindred,
and from thy father's house, unto the land that I will show thee.
And I will make of thee a great nation.*
Genesis 12 : 1–2

The patriarchs launched an idea of the greatest importance in human history – the belief in one God, known as monotheism. It was the Hebrews who established the first truly monotheistic creed.

The Hebrews were the first, too, to imagine a relationship based on an alliance or 'covenant' with a god who had no physical form and no name. It was this God who led Abraham to the promised land, Canaan, saying 'Unto thy seed will I give this land' (Genesis 12 : 7). Abraham undertook in return to serve him in total trust: this was the first alliance or 'covenant' between the people of Abraham and their God. This covenant was to be renewed by Isaac and Jacob, son and grandson of Abraham, and later by Moses.

Jacob's dream (15th century painting)
He dreamed, and behold a ladder set up on the earth, and the top of it reached to heaven; and, behold, the angels of God ascending and descending on it. And, behold, the Lord stood above it, and said, I am the Lord God of Abraham, thy father and the God of Isaac; the land whereon thou liest, to thee will I give it, and to thy seed . . . I am with thee, and will keep thee in all places whither thou goest.
Genesis 28 : 12–13, 15

As God could not be named (p. 22) Jewish tradition refers to him by an adjective, 'the Eternal'.

Abraham prepares to sacrifice his son Isaac at God's request. But God stops him: *Thou hast not withheld thy son, thine only son . . . I will bless thee and . . . I will multiply thy seed.* Genesis 22 : 16–17

137

And Mount Sinai was altogether on a smoke, because the Lord descended upon it in fire . . . and the whole mount quaked greatly . . . Moses spake, and God answered him by a voice.
Exodus 19 : 18–19

One of the routes thought to have been taken by the Israelites on leaving Egypt

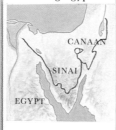

Moses receiving the Tables of the Law (13th century miniature)

The Founders

Moses passed on to the Hebrews the Law which still lies at the heart of Judaism. He freed the people of Israel from the bondage of slavery and led them for forty-years across the Sinai desert to the land of their ancestors, Canaan, the Promised Land.

During this long exodus he gave them the Tables of the Law, a charter summed up in the Ten Commandments. He also drew up rules governing every detail of daily life for Jews, and renewed the covenant between God and his people.

Arriving in Canaan, the people of Israel prospered.

Moses wrote all the words of the Lord. And he took the book of the covenant, and read in the audience of the people; and they said, All that the Lord hath said will we do, and be obedient.
Exodus 24 : 4, 7

They were ruled by kings, the most glorious of whom were David and his son, Solomon. They often fell into injustice and immorality, forgetting God, who sent them prophets to remind them of their promises.

A particularly testing time came with the destruction of Solomon's temple (586 BC) and the exile to Babylon. There, without the Ark or Temple, without a homeland or a king, they learned to live with their God as sole refuge and to obey his laws. Half a century later they returned from exile and rebuilt the Temple, while a scribe called Ezra organized the Israelites' religious lives, making them pay more attention to prayer, both at home and in the synagogue. The Second Temple was destroyed by the Romans in AD 70, and in 135 the Jews were dispersed throughout the world, so beginning what is known as the *diaspora*.

Second Temple in Jerusalem, built in 516 BC

Ark of the Covenant (bas-relief found in the ruins of Capernaum). The Law was carved on two tablets of stone placed in an ark which accompanied the Israelites to the Promised Land, and was then kept in the 'Holy of Holies' of the Temple in Jerusalem.

And the Lord went before them by day in a pillar of cloud to lead them the way, and by night in a pillar of fire, to give them light.
Exodus 13 : 21

Thou shalt have no other gods beside me.
Thou shalt not make unto thee any graven image.
Thou shalt not take the name of the Lord thy God in vain.
Remember the Sabbath day, to keep it holy.
Honour thy father and thy mother.
Thou shalt not kill. Exodus 20 : 3–13

'Bible' comes from the Greek *biblia*, a collection of books.

The Sanctuary of the Book houses the manuscripts discovered in 1947 near the Dead Sea. The scroll of the Book of Isaiah, a 1st century BC m.s. is one of the oldest known Hebrew texts of the Bible.

Texts

The whole of Jewish belief and tradition is expressed in a literature which extends from antiquity to the present day. It is written mainly in Hebrew, but also in Aramaic (once spoken in Palestine and Mesopotamia) and, in the Middle Ages, in Arabic.

The Hebrew Bible, or Written Law, is made up of 24 books composed at different times by authors who wrote down a body of knowledge which up till then had been passed on orally. These texts were collected in final form in the 10th century. The Bible is in three parts: The *Torah*, or Mosaic Law, also called *Pentateuch* from the

Celebration of the feast of *Simha Torah* in front of the west wall (remains of the Jerusalem Temple), called the 'Wailing Wall' by Christians. The reading of the *Torah* is done from a manuscript copy of the text made of parchment leaves stuck and sewn, end to end, then rolled round two wooden poles. This twin roll, the *Sefer-Torah*, is the holiest object in Judaism.

Greek word for 'five', is made up of five books: Genesis, Exodus, Leviticus, Numbers, and Deuteronomy, which ends with the death of Moses about 1200 BC; the *Books of the Prophets*; holy writings such as the *Psalms* (poems said to have been written by King David), the *Chronicles* and the *Proverbs*.

Supplementing the written law was the 'oral law' which was itself eventually written down as the *Mishna*. Later, a massive commentary, the *Gemara*, was added. These two together make up the *Talmud*, the main code of Jewish practice; the *Kabbalah* (or *Tradition*), is a mystical interpretation of the Law (p. 54), going back to antiquity. The most famous Kabbalistic work is the *Zohar* (or *Book of Splendour*).

Restoration work on manuscripts

יהוה

These four letters, or 'holy tetragram', symbolize the name of God; Jews are strictly forbidden to utter them and to write them.

This day the Lord thy God hath commanded thee to do these statutes and judgements; thou shalt therefore keep and do them with all thine heart, and with all thy soul.
Deuteronomy 26 : 16

This little leather box called the *tefillin* contains biblical verses copied on to parchment. Men can wear it tied on their forehead or left arm.

A boy's attaining religious majority at the age of 13 is marked by a ceremony, *Bar-Mitzvah*. He puts on the *talit*, the shawl fringed at its four corners recalling divine rules. Men must cover their heads during services. He fixes on his arm the *tefillin*, and reads a chapter from the Torah. From now on he is required to observe the rites and he is allowed to be one of the ten men needed for acts of public worship.

Ritual

Jewish daily life is governed by a number of practices and duties. The new-born child is given a Hebrew name during the recital of a prayer in the synagogue. Eight days after birth male children are circumcised: *Ye shall circumcise the flesh of your foreskin; and it shall be a token of the covenant betwixt me and you.* Genesis 17 : 11

At thirty days after his birth a boy is 'redeemed' by his father who gives the rabbi a silver coin, recalling in this way that the first-born of flocks were sacrificed to God and that the first-born of men were redeemed.

Below: a silver reading finger for following the sacred text, which may not be touched.

The *kipa* is a small cap which Jews wear on their heads as a token of their submission to God.

The *Sabbath* (from dusk on Friday to Saturday after dark) is a weekly festival which commemorates the way God rested on the seventh day after the Creation; mankind must do likewise. So on that day Jews do not utilize light or fire, cook, sew, write, handle money or use transport.

Food has to be correct: *kosher*. Animals that do not chew the cud (pigs and horses), fish without scales or fins, and animals slaughtered without having their throats cut and their blood drained, are all forbidden, and the health of animals is checked by a rabbi. Meat must not appear on the same menu as dairy products. All this would have had a sound hygienic basis during Jewish past history.

A rabbi blowing the *shofar*, a ram's horn, in memory of the animal sacrificed by Abraham instead of Isaac (p. 137)
'Sabbath' comes from the Hebrew word for 'rest'.
The *mezuzah* is a little piece of parchment in a metal case, with a passage from the *Torah*. It is fixed on the doors of the house.

A religious wedding can only take place where both partners are Jewish.

Seven days shalt thou eat unleavened bread, and on the seventh day shall be a feast to the Lord . . . And it shall be for a sign unto thee upon thine hand, and for a memorial between thine eyes, that the Lord's law may be in thy mouth; for with a strong hand hath the Lord brought thee out of Egypt.

Exodus 13 : 6, 9

During the feast of Passover, bitter herbs and unleavened bread are eaten to commemorate the slavery in Egypt and the wandering in the wilderness. On the first two evenings the *Seder* ceremony is a reminder of the last meal taken in captivity and is accompanied by the reading of the *Haggadah*, the story with commentary of the freeing of the Israelites (p. 136).

Festivals

In the Jewish calendar the years are numbered from the Creation, as the Bible indicates, so 1990, for instance, corresponds to the Jewish year 5750.

The year begins in autumn and is based on a lunar cycle of 354 days.

Pessah, Passover, lasting eight days, commemorates the flight from Egypt. It celebrates the renewal of the year.

Shavuoth or the Feast of the Weeks, seven weeks later, commemorates the gift of the *Torah*. It is the festival of first-fruits; synagogues are decorated with flowers, and the Ten Commandments and Book of Ruth are read.

The reading of the Torah accompanies all festivals.

Succoth, the Feast of the Booths, celebrates harvest. It recalls the wandering in the wilderness:

Ye shall dwell in booths seven days . . . that your generations may know that I made the children of Israel to dwell in booths, when I brought them out of the land of Egypt.
(Leviticus 23 : 42–43)

144

Rosh Ha-Shanah marks the start of the religious year and the ten days of repentance, during which a heavenly tribunal passes judgement on people. The prayers alternate with the blowing of the *shofar* (p. 143).

Rosh Ha-Shanah ends with *Yom kippur* or 'day of atonement', devoted to fasting and continuous prayer.

Huts with roofs of foliage are built in memory of divine protection in the wilderness. While prayers are being said a bundle of willow, myrtle and citron twigs is waved, symbolizing the unity of God's people in their diversity. On the eighth day the worshippers pray for rain. The ninth is *Simhat Torah* and closes the annual cycle of readings from the *Torah*.

Purim, or feast of lots, commemorates in the spring the deliverance of the Jews from Persia where they were threatened with extermination. It gives rise to acts of rejoicing and of charity; in Tel Aviv and New York carnivals fill the streets.

Hanukkah, festival of lights, recalls at the winter solstice the restoration of holy worship in the purified Temple (165 BC), following persecution by Greek colonizers. Every day for eight days a candle is lit on an eight-branched candlestick.

'Jew' means both a follower of Judaism, and one of the people of Israel.

145

*And yet for all that, when they be
in the land of their enemies,
I will not cast them away, neither will
I abhor them, to destroy them utterly.*
Leviticus 26 : 44

In several European
countries from the
Middle Ages onwards,
the *ghetto* was
a quarter or a street
where the Jews were
forced to live together.

The Jews in the World

From the first centuries AD the Jews were scattered: Babylon, Alexandria, Rome and the Mediterranean basin. Persecuted throughout their history, they went to Germany, England, France, Spain and Eastern Europe. Driven out again, they soon had only the choice of converting to Christianity or retreating to the ghetto (a quarter in a city where Jews were required to live). Pogroms (massacres) in Russia drove them to emigrate to the United States. Refugees from Nazism preferred to return to the land of their fathers: the state of Israel having been founded on 14 May 1948. Those who stay in the 'diaspora' (the dispersion) support the Israeli Jews while remaining loyal citizens of their adopted countries.

Israel has 3 million people, but the biggest Jewish community in the world is in the United States, with 6 million. Most are descended from Jews of Eastern Europe, *Ashkenazis*, who fled from persecution. There are just over 4 million Jews in Europe, half of them in the Soviet Union.

The Russian word *pogrom* refers to the acts of violence suffered by Jews in Poland and Russia in the late 19th century. The Jews were often forced to keep on the move, and so were known as a wandering people.

In 1933 Adolf Hitler, the founder of Nazism, took power in Germany and later launched a policy of systematic extermination of the Jews. Men, women and children were deported to concentration camps where they were held in appalling conditions before being executed. Six million died in this way.

There are several hundred thousand Jews in Britain. Some have been here for generations, while others came to England to escape persecution only recently.

Capture of the Warsaw ghetto by Hitler's troops in 1943

The return to the land of Israel is always symbolized by the planting of trees.

- 3 million (Israel)
- 6 million (USA)
- 500,000 to 2 million
- less than 500,000

Early Christianity

A 13th century mosaic of Christ. *Christ* is the Greek for *Messiah.*

In the 8th century BC, the Jewish prophet Isaiah (opposite) foretold the messiah's coming: *And the spirit of the Lord shall rest upon him, the spirit of wisdom and understanding, the spirit of counsel and might, the spirit of knowledge and of the fear of the Lord.*   Isaiah 11 : 2

Christianity is founded on the worship of Jesus of Nazareth.

Born in the reign of Herod the Great, Jesus grew up in Galilee, where he worked as a carpenter. When he was about 30 he began to preach, gathering round him a group of disciples in this remote region of Palestine.

Then, the Jewish people were living under foreign rule, either directly by Rome or by local princes appointed by the Roman Emperor. Divided amongst themselves, some accepted Roman rule, while others looked for the coming of a messiah, or king, to release them from servitude, as had been prophesied. Differences in religious beliefs made things worse. While the Jews worshipped one God (p. 137), the Greeks and Romans (p. 106) worshipped many.

Jesus, the Messiah.

To the people of his time Jesus offered something entirely new. He claimed to have a divine calling. He broke with tradition and gave fresh meaning to the Jewish scriptures, interpreting them with new insight in the name of God, whom he affectionately called *abba*, 'dear Father'.

His authority was heightened by extraordinary powers: stirring people's consciences, curing the sick and raising the dead.

He urged his followers to see the law as the expression of the will of God rather than a rigid set of rules to be obeyed to the letter: *the sabbath was made for man and not man for the sabbath.* Mark 2 : 27

He proclaimed the single most important rule for life to be love of God and of our fellow man. His life was a perfect example of this rule. The people to whom he ministered were the poor, the sick and those in need.

His actions

Jesus fired the crowds with enthusiasm, though many were disappointed that he did not call for the overthrow of their enemies.

He clashed with the Jewish religious leaders who refused to recognize him as a messenger of God. He was brought to trial at the time of the Passover in the year 30, condemned under Roman law and crucified. Two days later, according to Christian belief, Jesus rose from the dead and appeared to his disciples. This, the Resurrection, immeasurably strengthened the faith of the Christian community. Jesus' disciples were now certain that he was the long-awaited Messiah or Christ (anointed one) of the Jewish people, and the son of God.

And he goeth up into a mountain, and calleth unto him whom he would; and they came unto him.
Illustration taken from an 11th century Greek manuscript

Episodes in Christ's life: the Samaritan woman; healing lepers; curing a paralysed man.

*He whose sickness goes by the name of Jesus
may never be cured . . .*
Ibn al-Arabi, 13th century Muslim mystic

One of the early Christian symbols by which fellow Christians recognized each other was a fish.

Each of the evangelists is associated with a particular symbol, based on the winged figures from Ezekiel

Matthew: man

Mark: a lion

Luke: a bull

John: an eagle

The Written Word

Jesus left no written word of his teachings other than the existing Jewish scriptures (p. 140): the Law, the Prophets and writings which were considered in the lifetime of the apostles (Jesus' twelve disciples) to be the word of God.

An evangelist, inspired by God, dictating to a scribe (from an Armenian manuscript).

This is my commandment, That ye love
one another, as I have loved you.
St John 15 : 12

These writings were to be given the name *Old Testament*. They were studied and interpreted afresh as heralding the life and work of Jesus and the spirit of his message to mankind.

Before the death of the apostles and those others who had known Jesus, accounts of his life and of the early church were recorded and compiled to form the *New Testament*, written between AD 30 and 150. It consists of:

– The *Gospels*, a record of Jesus' ministry as remembered by those who knew him, written for the benefit of the Christian churches. There are four in all: St Mark's is the oldest and most down-to-earth; St Matthew, writing for fellow Jews, and St Luke for non-Jews (Gentiles). St John's Gospel, the last to be written, is more mystical and symbolic.

– The *Acts of the Apostles* describe the spread of Christianity beyond Israel.

– The *Epistles* were letters written by the heads of the churches to their communities to renew their faith, warn them against dangers and resolve their many problems.

– The *Revelation of John*, or *Apocalypse*, is a series of visions depicting the battle between the forces of good and evil, which predict the final triumph of the kingdom of God through Jesus Christ.

Fragment of a 4th century New Testament manuscript

The *Codex Sinaiticus*, a 4th century manuscript which contains the whole New Testament, was preserved in the monastery of St Catherine, in the Sinai desert.

*And they continued steadfastly in the apostles'
doctrine and fellowship and in breaking of bread,
and in prayers. And fear came upon every soul:
and many wonders and signs were done by the apostles.*
Acts of the Apostles 2 : 42–3

*But the word of God
grew and multiplied.*
Acts of the Apostles 12 : 24

Painting found in
a catacomb,
probably showing
an Apostle

Paul's missionary
journeys and the
first Christian
communities
– in white: Paul's
first journey;
– in orange: Paul's
second journey;
– in blue: Paul's
third journey.

The persecution of
Christians ended
only in AD 313.

The spread of Christianity

Jesus had gathered disciples around
him and entrusted them with spread-
ing the Gospel to all parts of the world.

The first step was the establishment
of the church in Jerusalem. Many Jews
joined the disciples, causing the Jewish
leaders to persecute them. The disciples and their converts scattered, foun-
ding small groups of Christians around
the Mediterranean, and attracting
members who were not Jewish.

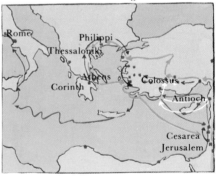

Rome
Philippi
Thessaloniki
Athens
Corinth
Colossus
Antioch
Cesarea
Jerusalem

As more churches sprang up a new
generation of leaders took over: they
were the Church fathers such as
Irenaeus, Origen, and Tertullian.
When Roman persecution ceased,
theologians such as John Chrysostom,
Jerome and Augustine began to define
Christianity as a religion. The great
councils of the churches decided
questions of doctrine and established
Christian beliefs.

> *For as the body is one, and has many members, and all the members*
> *of that one body, being many, are one body; so also is Christ.*
> *For by one Spirit are we all baptized into one body, whether we be*
> *bond or free; and have been all made to drink into one Spirit.*
> 1st Epistle of Paul to the Corinthians 12 : 12–13

Breaking bread and sharing food were symbols of fellowship and love between early Christians. (From a 3rd century Roman tomb)

The role played by Paul

– He showed that Christianity went far beyond the promises of the Old Testament. It was a new stage in the relationship between God and man, destined not just for a chosen few, but for all humanity.

– He based his teachings on Christ's life and work. The son of God came to deliver man from his sins. By accepting death on the cross Jesus offered the one perfect sacrifice to his Father; through his resurrection he promised new life to all who follow him.

– Paul was responsible for carrying the Good News throughout the eastern half of the Roman Empire and to Rome itself.

The apostles Peter and Paul, from a 16th century icon.

Paul brought home to his followers the novelty of Christianity as a way of life. A strictly Orthodox Jew (Pharisee) until his conversion to Christianity in AD 37, he thereafter devoted all his time and prodigious energy to promoting the spread of Christianity.

The first Christians formed close-knit communities in which possessions were shared equally, following Christ's example and teaching.

Orthodoxy

Russian Orthodox
Cross

A *schism* is a split or
divide between people
of the same religion.

The Christian comm-
unities which main-
tained the *dogmas*
(p. 248) established
at the Ecumenical
Councils were called
orthodox (in Greek,
sound in doctrine) and
catholic (meaning
general, universal).

The Orthodox churches did not
suddenly spring up in 1054, the year of
the Great Schism between East and
West. They evolved from the early
Christian communities, and had
already existed for centuries.

The style of worship varied according to local customs and traditions.
Each regional church was represented
at the Ecumenical councils by its own
bishop. Those of the five major cities
(who were called patriarchs) recognized the primacy of the Church of
Jerusalem, followed by that of Rome.

In the 11th century the Bishop of
Rome decided to change the nature of
this authority. He wanted Rome to
have power of jurisdiction over all
Christian communities. The majority
of the Eastern churches opposed this

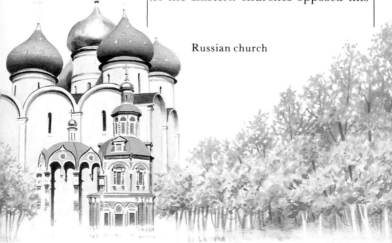

Russian church

decision. The only universal authority they would accept was an Ecumenical council.

The Christians of Western Europe supported the bishop of Rome, which is why they became known as Roman Catholics. The other churches kept the name *Orthodox*. They are catholic, but not Roman Catholic.

An icon is a picture painted in accordance with certain rules which seeks to convey a spiritual message in a stylized form. God the Father is never depicted in person but is seen in the figures of Jesus, Mary and the saints. Icon painting is an art which has been handed down over the centuries. *Abraham's Hospitality*, painted by the Russian monk, Rublyov, in the 14th century, is one of the most famous.

Greek church

Vladimir of Kiev, founder of the Russian Orthodox church, was converted in 988.

Greek Orthodox cross

Ethiopian Orthodox cross

155

*The ultimate aim of the Christian life
is to receive the Holy Spirit of God.
The grace of the Holy Spirit is Light.*
Seraphim of Sarov, 19th century
Russian monk and saint

Hermits (from the
Greek *eremos*, desert)
lead a solitary life,
away from the world.

*And the desert became a
city, peopled with monks
who had renounced their
worldly goods, and
enrolled instead as
citizens of Heaven.*
4th century Life
of Antony

Worship

At home and in church, Orthodox
Catholics stand to pray. During the
church service they sing, process, light
candles, bow low, kiss the icons, and
cross themselves. Worship occupies a
very important place in the Orthodox
tradition.

Religious services consist of prayer,
readings from the Bible, and the
Eucharist (p. 33). The liturgy conveys
the Gospel message to four of the
senses: to the ear, in chanting; to taste
(in the bread which is blessed and
passed round); to the nose, in the
incense; to the eye (the candelabra,
sumptuous liturgical vestments and
icons).

The clergy

– Priests, assisted by deacons,
preside over all the religious
services.

– Bishops, responsible for small
communities, are known affectionately as *Pape* (Papa). Each national
church has its own patriarch and
regional bishops or metropolitans.

– The ecumenical patriarch of
Constantinople is the leading figure
of the whole church, but his
authority is not absolute. He is 'first
among equals'. All decisions are
taken in assemblies (*synods*).

Around the 4th and 5th cent. some
Eastern monks withdrew from the
world and became known as the
Desert Fathers.